AF560714

World Trade Organisation and Economic Growth

By

Dr. M. Lakshmi Narasaiah

M.A., Ph.D.

Professor of Economics,
Co-ordinator, Department of M.B.A. and Commerce,
Special Officer,
Sri Krishnadevaraya University Post-graduate Centre,
Kurnool–518 002
Andhra Pradesh (India)

DISCOVERY PUBLISHING HOUSE
NEW DELHI

First Published–2006

ISBN: 81-8356-081-4

Published by:

DISCOVERY PUBLISHING HOUSE

4831/24, Prahlad Street, Ansari Road, Darya Ganj
New Delhi–110 002 (India)
Phone: 23279245, • Fax: 91-11-23253475
e-mail: dphtemp@indiatimes.com

Printed at
Arora Offset Press
Laxmi Nagar, Delhi–92

Preface

The successful conclusion of the Uruguay Round was the most significant economic event of 1994. The Round contributed to liberalisation of trade in goods, services and investment. It represents a decisive step towards introducing market solutions in international transactions. It entails significant potential gains for the world economy. But the distribution of gains across regions, nations and various groups within countries will be uneven, giving rise to certain challenges and risks. These merit the attention of the international community.

The process of trade liberalisation intensifies the trend towards globalisation. Free movements of goods and services across countries will mean greater mobility of capital and foreign direct investment. These factors taken together should contribute to the efficiency of the world economy by encouraging countries to produce goods and services in which they hold a comparative advantage. International competition on price and quality will thus intensify, leading to the development of new products and processes.

The downside of this process is, however, that it can accelerate two other trends. The first is the concentration of market structures, both at the global and national levels. The role of transnational corporations in the world economy is increasing, and while much stress is justifiably laid on promoting small and medium sized enterprises, there is no doubt that big business will have a growing role in economic activities not only in developed but also in developing countries. Even if measures are taken to prevent, through competition policy, possible abuses of dominant positions by large enterprises, the trend towards concentration of market power through globalisation will continue to have important implications for world trade and production.

The second trend is towards the potential marginalisation of poor nations and vulnerable groups within nations. The least developed countries, particularly in sub-Saharan Africa, for example, will experience losses in the short and even medium term as a result of the Uruguay Round agreements. They lack sufficient supply capacity to produce and export goods for which market access has improved. More importantly, they will not be able to exercise policy options that were available to the newly industrialized countries during their early development stage. Further, their competitive position in the world economy might be weakened with the new trends towards regionalism, as well as new methods of production.

Conversely, the intensification of international competition will inevitably enhance the position of the most efficient producers, with implications for the location of industries, and hence for employment. This will add fuel to the arguments of the advocates of protectionism.

Therefore, although the world economy as a whole benefits from trade liberalisation, there are risks of marginalisation which may lead to tensions among nations and among various groups within them and eventually could result in trade conflicts, undermining the security of the international trading system. The threat of instability of the trading system arises, in a sense, from a sort of "prisoners dilemma", whereby the common interests of the universe as a whole may diverge from the perceived individual interests of the main participating countries. Countries have a common interest in liberalizing international trade. However, individual countries may feel their interest lies in restricting trade so as to, inter alia, "protect" jobs. The balance could then be tipped in favour of protectionism, either overt or disguised as anti-dumping measures or environmental criteria and health and labour standards applied unilaterally. Likewise, the argument for the protection of strategic industries may be invoked.

As the invisible hand of the market by itself is insufficient to bring about social justice at the national level, market forces alone are equally incapable of preserving the common interest of all nations in a globalized world economy. A liberalized global economy requires a suitable framework of governance and institutions. In particular, like the need for a social safety net at the national level to avert social conflicts, there is also a need for a safety net at the international level to prevent the weakening of the international trading system, the environmental commons and peaceful international relations. Our existing institutional set-ups tend to lag behind economic changes, both at the national and international levels.

Dr. M. Lakshmi Narasaiah

Contents

The WTO is Born

Affirming that "the establishment of the World Trade Organisation (WTO) ushers in a new era of global economic cooperation, reflecting the widespread desire to operate in a fairer and more open multilateral trading system for the benefit and welfare of their people," more than a hundred ministers in the ancient trading crossroads of Marrakesh signed the Final Act of the Uruguay Round and made decisions ensuring a running start for the WTO.

In the ornate Salle Royale of the Palaisdes Congress, the ministers, one by one, signed the Final Act containing 28 agreements and appended to by some 26,000 pages of national tariff and services schedules, which GATT economists estimate will add some US $755 billion to world exports and raise incomes by some $235 billion annually.

Several ministers also signed the new Government Procurement Code that was negotiated in parallel with the Uruguay Round and three other plurilateral agreements: on dairy products, bovine meat and civil aircraft. The ceremony effectively marked the start of the transition from GATT to the WTO.

In the Marrakesh Declaration they had adopted just hours earlier, the Ministers had saluted as "a historic achievement" the conclusion of the round, which strengthen the world economy, lead to more trade, investment, employment and income growth throughout the world". They had also expressed their determination to "resist protectionist pressures of all kinds". In this regard, they pledged, with immediate effect and until the establishment of the WTO, not to "take any trade measures that would undermine or adversely affect the results of the Uruguay Round negotiations or their implementation."

Ministerial Decisions

The establishment of a Preparatory Committee for the WTO was one of the four decisions taken by ministers. The other three were: the Decision on Acceptance of the Accession to the Agreement Establishing the World Trade Organisation; the Decision on Trade and Environment; and the Decision on Organisational and Financial Consequences flowing from Implementation of the Agreement Establishing the WTO.

The Preparatory Committee, to be headed by Mr. Peter Sutherland in his personal capacity, will be in charge of ensuring an orderly transition from the GATT to the WTO. Its remit is to ensure the efficient operation of the WTO immediately as of the date of its establishment. Thus, it will convene and prepare the Implementation Conference, which will decide formally on the date of entry into force of the WTO Agreement.

Opening Ceremonies

"Our meeting here in Marrakesh takes place at the close of the most ambitious trade negotiations in world economic history—we should be proud of this stride towards a more open world which will be, through the dynamism of exchanges between nations and the lifting of barriers and protectionist regulations, a source of prosperity and welfare for the people worldwide," said His Royal Highness the Crown Prince Sidi Mohammed at the opening of the Ministerial Meeting. He stressed that "we all are witnessing here in Marrakesh what will be the legal and institutional pillar of International Trade in the twenty-first century."

The TNC Chairman at Ministerial level, Minister Sergio Abreau Bonilla (Uruguay), opened the Ministerial

Meeting by reminding participants that the real effectiveness of the new trade rules depended on the political will of governments. "We must therefore strengthen our determination to honour the commitments which we will assume with the signature of the Final Act," he said. Minister Abreau added: "Behind each signature, there are millions of workers, farmers, industrialists, professionals and businessmen who harbour the hope that the results of the Round will create new horizons for trade, employment and investment and offer better possibilities of tackling poverty and recession, the paving the way for the economic and social development of nations."

Sutherland's Report

"Few trading caravans can have viewed this beautiful city with as much pleasure and as much relief—as ours does. But then very few trading caravans were on the road for more than seven years, and none carried such a priceless cargo. This week you as Ministers will sign the greatest trade agreement in history, one whose benefits span entire continents and a wide range of trade sectors alike," the TNC Chairman at Officials Level, GATT Director-General Peter Sutherland said.

Mr. Sutherland reported that the work of the TNC since the successful conclusion of the Uruguay Round negotiations on 15 December 1993 had been focused on the preparations for the Marrakesh Meeting. First, the Final Act Embodying the Results of the Uruguay Round of Multilateral Trade Negotiations was legally rectified, agreed and circulated to all participants. Secondly, the schedules of market access commitments in goods and services and the MFN exemption lists in services were multilaterally verified for attachment to the Marrakesh Protocol. Thus the Final Act, rectified and completed by the verified schedules, was now well as trade and investment.

Reflecting on the successful conclusion of the negations, US Trade Representative Michael Kantor said he was "struck by the thin line that separates success and failure... (but) we succeeded because the ties that bind us together are strong than the forces seeking to pull us apart." He stressed that "our vision of the trading system must be dynamic and able to meet the emerging challenges to our collective global economic growth." Thus, "increasingly, we will address issues related to each other's internal policies, such as competition policy and other domestic regulatory policies, as well as environmental protection and labour standards."

Canada's Trade Minister, Mr. Roy MacLaren, emphasised that when WTO is asked to tackle new trade policy issues, it should proceed in a manner consistent with its competence and mandate. He warned that "when examining new issues, we must, for example be wary of being seduced by the argument that differing approaches to issues such as environmental protection constitute an unfair trade practice justifying some form of action—new issues can become a vehicle for new protectionism." Minister MacLaren stressed that "to fall victim in the World Trade Organisation to the narrow interest groups who favour trade sanctions as the instrument of choice to force nations to comply with the policies of other would be to abandon some of the most fundamental gains we have made."

Development Goals

India's Minister of Commerce, Mr. Pranab Mukherjee, warned that the acute differences between levels of development and incomes among nations have "enough latent heat to melt down the most elaborately engineered structures." Thus, "the long-term survival of the multilateral trading system will depend upon reducing the present inequities." Regarding new issues, Minister Mukherjee said, while India was strongly committed to internationally-recognised labour standards, it could not see any merit in linking this subject to international trade. On the other hand, he attached importance to an examination in the Preparatory Committee of the relationship between immigration policies and international trade.

Bangladesh' Minister for Commerce, Mr. M. Shamsul Islam, speaking on behalf of the least-developed countries, hoped that "in the implementation of the Uruguay Round Agreements, the international community will be more responsive to the needs of the most disadvantaged group of nations." He urged a comprehensive assessment of the Uruguay Round results with "any imbalances ... to be redressed through appropriate action including additional trade preferences, development assistance and debt relief." Minister Islam pointed to the "need by LLDCS for substantial technical assistance in the implementation of the results of the Round. On new issues, he supported the consideration of the relationship between movements of natural persons and international trade in the Preparatory Committee.

Zimbabwe's Minister of Industry and Commerce, Dr. H. Murerwa, said that his country's preliminary evaluation of the Uruguay Round results suggested gains for certain products, stand–still position for others and potential losses for some products as a result of erosion of EC trade preferences. However, he believed that "the process of liberalisation will in the long–run strengthen the global trading system and benefit the peoples of both the developed and developing countries." Minister Murerwa said the challenge facing the developing countries is "to expand and diversify our export capabilities as well as strengthening the international competitiveness of our products." Re-ready for signature by Ministers. Simultaneously, the TNC at official level had approved for adoption by Ministers four Decisions and the Marrakesh Declaration.

The GATT Director-General said that "the signature ceremony will be a just cause for celebration not only because it represents signing-off on the Uruguay Round, but because it will be signing-on to the work of putting the results into effect and ensuring that their potential is used to the fullest."

Early Ratification Urged

Many Ministers underlined the urgency of ratifying the Uruguay Round agreements to enable the World Trade Organisation to be fully operational.

EC Commissioner Sir Leon Brittan emphasised that: "each of us, by our signature at Marrakesh, pledges himself or herself to submit the results of the Uruguay Round for formal approval in accordance with our domestic laws and, equally important, to proceed without delay to implement in our domestic laws, the commitments we made during the negotiations" He said one proof of the quality of those commitments was "the ever-lengthening queue of candidates for accession to the GATT and to the WTO." The EC Commissioner suggested that the WTO tackle the following issues: ensuring intensive cooperation between the WTO and the IMF and the World Bank; addressing urgently the interface between trade and the environment; working with the International Labour Office and other organisations, the WTO must address problems such as child exploitation, forced labour or the denial to workers of free speech or free association; and distortion of trade which can be caused by different standards of competition law and practice in different countries.

Japan's Deputy Prime Minister and Minister for Foreign Affairs Mr. Tsutomu Hata, underlined the importance of the Round's conclusion "in securing confidence in the world economic order." He recalled that his country had made significant contributions to the Round, including acceptance of the Agreement on Agriculture and cutting average tariffs on industrial and mining products by 61 per cent to rate as low as 1.5 per cent. "As a result of the Uruguay Round, the Japanese market offers greater opportunities for success by foreign exporters depending upon their efforts," he added. Minister Hata expressed strong support for the early entry into force of the WTO Agreement, and suggested that the WTO consider additional issues closely related to trade, including regionalism as grading the WTO, he viewed "Marrakesh as the stating platform which will put in place a strong rule-based multilateral trading system that should safeguard the interest of all nations, weak and strong."

The Swiss Minister of Public Economy, Mr. J.P. Delamuraz, pointed out that "by concluding the Uruguay Round, we have taken a decisive step towards the adaptation of the multilateral trading system to contemporary economic realities." This had meant for many participant "substantial adjustments" in domestic economic policy, and for Switzerland reforms in its agricultural policy. "We have added a number of stones to the foundations of a system of multilateral management of the world economy," said Mr. Delamuraz, "we have also recognised the interdependence that is binding us ever more closely together." He noted with special satisfaction the confirmation in the Marrakesh Declaration of the "need for positive measures on behalf of the developing countries, and especially of the least developed among them, as well as the desirability of possible additional measures for their benefit." Mexico's Secretary for Trade and Industrial Development, Mr. Jaime Serra Puche, lauded the result of the Round as signifying "recognition" of the adjustment measures that have been taken up by many developing countries to open their economies. He believed that the results "will further the creation of new jobs and growth in the wage levels of our workers." Secretary Puche stressed that "protection of the environment and workers' rights must go hand in hand with efforts to liberalise world trade, for progress in liberalisation to improve the environment and the well-being of workers," but warned against these subject being used as pretexts for "disguised trade protectionism."

Brazil's Minister of External Relations, Mr. Celso Amorium, said that the Uruguay Round "will be remembered as the first one in which developing countries had an active participation in the course of the whole negotiating process." He underlined that "We, the developing countries, have bet on trade liberalisation and on the multilateral trading system... Even though our organisation does not bear the word development in its name, it will lose much of its purpose if its rules and disciplines do not contribute to freeing hundreds of millions of human beings from poverty and misery."

The Czech Republic's Minister of Industry and Trade, Mr. Vladimir Dlouhy, highlighted the importance his country attached to "the full integration of the economies in transition into the multilateral trading system." Pointing to these countries' need for better access to markets and fair application of trade and competition rules, he urged that "the role of the multilateral trading system in this process should be made more effective and more visible."

Singapore's Minister for Trade and Industry, Mr. Yeo Cheow Tong, said "the signing of the Final Act does not mean the end ... the challenge now is to see through the successful establishment of the WTO and the implementation of the agreement." Minister Yeo said that Singapore fully supported the WTO because it "has long recognised that the free market system is the way to economic growth and prosperity for our people." In line with this, he extended his country's invitation to host the first Ministerial Meeting of the WTO. "This will be the first time a major global trade meeting will be held in Asia, and will complete the circle of Uruguay Round meetings that began in South America in Uruguay, then moved on to the North America, to Europe and today in Marrakesh, Africa," he added.

Conclusion

At the conclusion of the Ministerial Meeting Minister Abreau noted that many of the one hundred ministers who have spoken had stressed that "notwithstanding the tumultuous economic and political events of the past seven-and-a-half years, all participants have undertaken considerable efforts to improve conditions of market access." Noteworthy too had been "the engagement of the developing and least-developed countries in the process of countributing their share to the global effort to reduce trade barriers."

Another major theme was "the role that multilateral cooperation must play as the foundation for trade relations amongst nations." Minister Abreau said that to implement this principle on a permanent basis, "all had agreed that the results of the negotiations constituted a single undertaking, based on the WTO as a new international institution." He added that one decision taken at the meeting was the convening of an Implementation Conference later in the year.

In the course of the meeting, the TNC Chairman said ministries had stressed the importance they attached to the examination in the Preparatory Committee of the following subjects for inclusion in the WTO agenda: the relationship between the trading system and internationally recognised labour standards; the relationship between immigration policies and international trade; trade and competition policy, including rules on export financing and restrictive business practices; trade and investment; regionalism; the interaction between trade policies and policies relating to financial and monetary matters, including debt and commodity markets; international trade and company law; the establishment of a mechanism for compensation for the erosion of preferences; the link between trade, development, political stability and the alleviation of poverty; and unilateral or extraterritorial trade measures.

2

What is the WTO?

The World Trade Organisation (WTO) will facilitate the implementation and operation of all the agreements and legal instruments negotiated in connection with the Uruguay Round, including the Plurilateral Trade Agreements (trade in civil aircraft, government procurement, trade in dairy products and bovine meat); it will provide a forum for all negotiations; and it will administer the Understanding on Rules and Procedures Governing the Settlement of Disputes and the Trade Policy Review Mechanism (TPRM). It will cooperate with the International Monetary Fund and the International Bank for Reconstruction and Development with a view to achieving greater coherence in global economic policy-making.

In its Preamble, the Agreement establishing a World Trade Organisation reiterates the objectives of the GATT, namely raising standard of living and incomes, ensuring full employment, expanding production and trade, and optimal use of the world's resources, while at the same time extending them to services and making them more precise:

- It introduces the idea of "sustainable development" in relation to the optimal use of the world's resources, and the need to protect and preserve the environment in a manner consistent with the various levels of national economic development.

- It recognizes that there is a need for positive efforts designed to ensure that developing countries, and especially the least-developed among them, secure a better share of the growth in international trade.

Decision-making

The WTO will continue the decision-making practice followed under the GATT: decision by consensus which is deemed to exist if no member formally objects. Recourse to voting, where a decision cannot be reached by consensus, is institutionalised, whereas previously it was exceptional. Decision will still be taken by a majority of the votes cast, on the basis of "one country one vote".

However, in two cases—interpretation of the provisions of the agreements and waiver of a member's obligations—conditions imposed by the Agreement and more severe. The majority required is then three-quarters of the members, whereas under the GATT it was only two-thirds of the votes cast representing at least half of the members. Moreover, the granting of waivers will be more strictly controlled (justification, time-limits, possibility of recourse to dispute settlement).

Any member of the WTO may submit a proposal to amend the provisions of the Agreements to the Ministerial Conference and the General Council. The quorum necessary to implement changes will depend on the nature of the amendment:

- amendments relating to general principles such as MFN treatment, must be approved by all members;
- for all other amendments only a two-thirds majority is required.

Original and New Members

The member countries of the GATT as of the date of entry into force of the WTO Agreement will become original members of the WTO. However, the least-developed countries recognised as such by the United Nations will only be required to undertake commitments and concessions to the extent consistent with their individual development.

The accession procedures and the majority of two-thirds of the members required remain the same as under the GATT.

Status and Budget

The WTO will have legal personality and will be accorded privileges and immunities similar to those accorded to the specialised agencies of the United Nations. The Status of the GATT was relatively ambiguous because of the failure to set up an International Trade Organisation in 1947. Formally, the GATT is a multilateral treaty administered by an Interim Committee.

The establishment of the World Trade Organisation will reinforce the status and the image of the principal institution with responsibility for international trade, by placing it on the same footing as the IMF and the World Bank.

The Director-General of the WTO will be appointed by the Ministerial Conference which will also adopt regulations setting up his power and duties.

The financial regulations relating to the scale of contributions and the budget will be based on the rules and practices of the GATT.

Entry into Force

The Agreement was opened for acceptance by signature at Marrakesh and will enter into force by 1 January 1995 or as early as possible thereafter; the precise date will be fixed by a ministerial conference when most countries are in a position to give a commitment with respect to their date of ratification.

An original member accepting the Agreement after its entry into force will have to implement those concessions and obligations that are to be implemented over a period of time as if it had accepted the Agreement on the date of its entry into force.

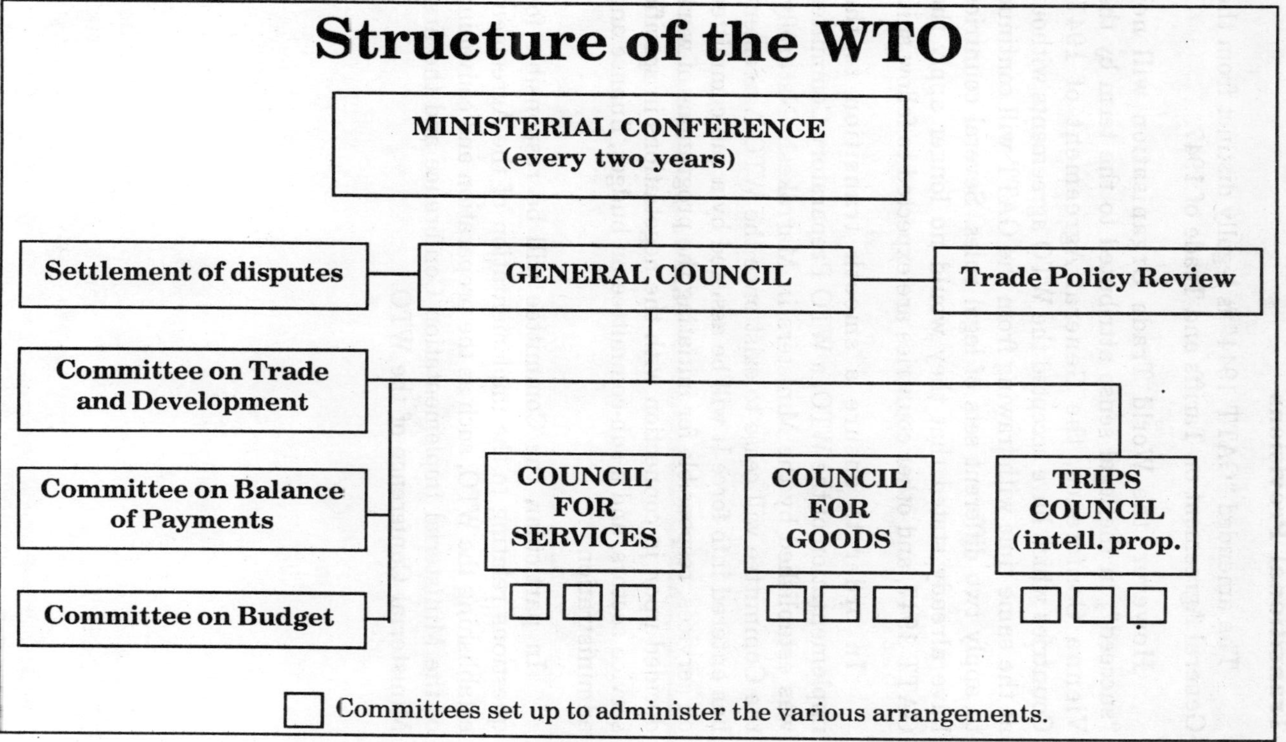
Structure of the WTO
MINISTERIAL CONFERENCE
(every two years)
Settlement of disputes
GENERAL COUNCIL
Trade Policy Review
Committee on Trade and Development
Committee on Balance of Payments
Committee on Budget
COUNCIL FOR SERVICES
COUNCIL FOR GOODS
TRIPS COUNCIL (intell. prop.
Committees set up to administer the various arrangements.

Transitional Provisions

The amended "GATT 1944" is legally distinct from the General Agreement on Tariffs and Trade of 1947.

However, the World Trade Organisation will not "succeed", in the legal sense attributed to the term by the Vienna Conference, the General Agreement of 1947. Countries which have accepted the WTO agreements without at the same time withdrawing from the GATT will continue to apply two different sets of legal rules. Several countries have already stated that they would no longer apply the GATT 1947, and other countries are expected to follow suit.

In order to ensure a smooth transition to the implementation of the WTO, a WTO Preparatory Committee was established by the Ministers in Marrakesh. Naturally, the Committee will cease to exist once the WTO Agreement has entered into force It will be assisted by a sub-committee on services, responsible for initiating the programme of work decided upon in connection with the negotiations in specific service sectors, and a sub-committee on budget, finance and administration.

In particular, the Committee will be responsible for questions relating to the implementation of the Agreement establishing the WTO, such as the preparation and convening of the Ministerial Implementation Conference and the first Ministerial Conference of the WTO.

3

Beyond the Uruguay Round

Opportunities and Challenges

The successful conclusion of the Uruguay Round was the most significant economic event of 1994. The Round contributed to liberalisation of trade in goods, services and investment. It represents a decisive step towards introducing market solutions in international transactions. It entails significant potential gains for the world economy. But the distribution of gains across regions, nations and various groups within countries will be uneven, giving rise to certain challenges and risks. These merit the attention of the international community.

The process of trade liberalisation intensifies the trend towards globalisation. Free movements of goods and services across countries will mean greater mobility of capital and foreign direct investment. These factors taken together should contribute to the efficiency of the world economy by encouraging countries to produce goods and services in which they hold a comparative advantage. International competition on price and quality will thus intensify, leading to the development of new products and processes.

The downside of this process is however, that it can accelerate two other trends. The first is the concentration of market structures, both at the global and national levels. The role of transnational corporations in the world economy is increasing, and while much stress is justifiably laid on promoting small and medium sized enterprises, there is no doubt that big business will have a growing role in economic activities not only in developed but also in developing countries. Even if measures are taken to prevent, through competition policy, possible abuses of dominant positions by large enterprises, the trend towards concentration of market power through globalisation will continue to have important implications for world trade and production.

The second trend is towards the potential marginalisation of poor nations and vulnerable groups within nations. The least developed countries, particularly in sub-Saharan Africa, for example, will experience losses in the short and even medium term as a result of the Uruguay Round agreements. They lack sufficient supply capacity to produce and export goods for which market access has improved. More importantly, they will not be able to exercise policy options that were available to the newly industrialised countries during their early development stage. Further, their competitive position in the world economy might be weakened with the new trends towards regionalism, as well as new methods of production.

Conversely, the intensification of international competition will inevitably enhance the position of the most efficient producers, with implications for the location of industries, and hence for employment. This will add fuel to the arguments of the advocates of protectionism.

Therefore, although the world economy as a whole benefits from trade liberalisation, there are risks of marginalisation which may lead to tensions among nations and among various groups within them and eventually could result in trade conflicts, undermining the security of the international trading system. The threat of instability of the trading system arises, in a sense, from a sort of "prisoners dilemma", whereby the common interests of the universe as a whole may diverge from the perceived individual interests of the main participating countries. Countries have a common interest in liberalizing international trade. However, individual countries may feel their interest lies in restricting trade so as to, inter alia, "protect" jobs. The balance could then be tipped in favour of protectionism, either overt or disguised as anti-dumping measures or environmental criteria and health and labour standards applied unilaterally. Likewise, the argument for the protection of strategic industries may be invoked.

As the invisible hand of the market by itself is insufficient to bring about social justice at the national level, market forces alone are equally incapable of preserving the common interest of all nations in a globalised world economy. A liberalised global economy requires a suitable framework of governance and institutions. In particular, like the need for a social safety net at the national level to avert social conflicts, there is also a need for a safety net at the international level to prevent the weakening of the international trading system, the environmental commons and peaceful international relations. Our existing institutional set-ups tend to lag behind economic changes, both at the national and international levels.

At the national level there is need for strengthening the social mechanisms and to pay closer attention to the distributional aspects of the benefits of production and trade; this is also true at the international level. Furthermore, there is a need for strengthening the socio-economic functions in order to find pragmatic solutions to universal problems arising from change and to preserve the common interests of people everywhere. Sound analysis is called for in this regard. A creative approach is needed, departing as necessary from conventional views, and aimed at arriving at commitments implementable by all.

4

The WTO and the Developing Countries

The special status of developing countries in the GATT will continue to receive recognition in the WTO. The preamble of the Agreement Establishing the WTO states that "there is a need for positive efforts designed to ensure that developing countries, and especially the least developed among them, secure a share in the growth of international trade commensurate with the needs of their economic development". In addition to retaining the provisions that concerned developing countries in GATT 1947, the new agreement generally contain provisions for developing countries and least-developed countries, often consisting of longer transition periods for the full implementation of some obligations and various exemptions from obligations, particularly for the latter group of countries. Also, in some instances, the exports of developing countries benefit from a better treatment with respect to measures taken by other WTO members. Technical assistance is to be provided to developing countries to assist them in assuming their obligations and more effectively realizing the benefits of the multilateral trading system.

Least-developed countries are singled out in the Final Act as requiring special attention. This is reflected in the agreements through a number of provisions which provide the most favourable treatment for this group in terms of rights as well as lower levels of obligations. In addition, the Decision on Measures in Favour of Least-Developed Countries, makes provision for measures of special assistance, including technical assistance "in the development, strengthening and diversification of their production and export bases including those of services, as well as in trade promotion, to enable them to maximize the benefits from liberalised access to markets". As part of its functions, the Committee on Trade and Development (a subsidiary body of the General Council) will periodically review the special provisions in favour of least-developed countries and report to the General Council of the WTO for appropriate action.

The Declaration on the Contribution of the WTO to Achieving Greater Coherence in Global Economic Policy making identifies the need for strengthening the relationship between the activities of the WTO, the International Monetary Fund (IMF) and the World Bank as a way of ensuring greater coherence in global economic policy-making.

Market Access

Industrial Products: For developed countries, the main features of their market access commitments in industrial products include the expansion of bindings to cover 99 per cent of imports; the expansion of duty free access from 30 to 44 per cent of total imports; and the reduction of the trade-weighted average tariff by 40 per cent (i. e. from the pre-Uruguay Round level of 6.2 per cent to the post-Uruguay Round level of 3.7 per cent). With respect to tariff reductions on individual product categories, developed countries will reduce tariffs by substantially above-average amounts (60 per cent or more) in three categories—wood, pulp, paper and furniture; metals; and non-electric machinery and reduce tariffs by less than the 40 per cent overall reduction in four categories—fish and fish products; textiles and clothing; leather, rubber, footwear; and transport equipment.

In terms of exports from developing to developed country markets, the total reduction in the average tariff of developed countries is 37 per cent. Below average tariff reductions, and above-average levels of tariffs apply to labour-intensive manufacturers (textiles and clothing, leather goods) and certain processed primary products (fish products) that have been—and continue to be—regarded as "sensitive".

Developed countries constitute the most important merchandise exports market for developing countries (62 per cent in 1992). In part, this is because the developed countries account for the bulk of global income and expenditures. At the same time, market access opportunities for developing countries in each other's markets have long been affected by the protection in their own markets. In many instances, the level of protection is quite high, because important protection, ultimately, acts as a tax on exports as well, protection in developing countries also hinders the integration of developing economies, not just with each other, but with the larger global trading system.

The reductions in bound tariffs which the new commitments of developing economies represent are difficult to assess for several reasons. The first is that comprehensive information on base (1986) tariffs is unavailable in many cases as a result of the low level of bindings among developing countries. In these cases, the post-Uruguay Round average bound tariff usually involves a decrease in the ceiling bindings applied to items already found, combined with ceiling bindings above currently applied rates for previously unbound items. Another reason is that, where developing economies had bound all or a significant portion of tariffs prior to the end of the Round, the Uruguay Round tariff commitments often reflect a decline in ceiling rates (rather than applied rates).

At the same time, current tariff levels already reflect the often substantial reductions undertaken autonomously in the course of the Round. Though many developing countries may not be required to introduce further cuts, previous liberalisation has been at least partly locked in through new commitments on bindings. Ceiling bindings are considered to be so important that countries which agree to bind previously unbound tariffs are given "negotiating credits" for the decision even if the tariff is bound at a level above the currently applied level (as is the case for many developing economy participants in the Round). Bindings have also played a key role in establishing the domestic and international credibility of domestic reform programmes in many countries. Although an integral part of the tariff negotiations, bindings clearly are more akin to rules and procedures—in terms of their contribution to the predictability of future market access—than to direct increases in market access. However, even ceiling bindings yield significant benefits related to liberalisation when they reduce the expect value and variance of protection.

On the basis of data available for 26 developing countries, the GATT Secretariat has identified the main features of their market access commitments. These include: the expansion of bindings to cover 61 per cent of imports, compared to the pre-Uruguay Round level of 13 per cent. The increase in the security of trade among developing regions is reflected mainly in Latin America—where participants will bind 100 per cent of tariff lines at ceilings rates.

Too often, "market access" as used in descriptions of the Uruguay Round results is defined—implicitly or explicitly in a way that is too narrow and, even worse, mercantilist. The narrowness results from limiting the analysis of changes in market access to changes in tariffs and quotas. This overlooks three other key aspects of market access, namely the bindings of tariffs, the rules and disciplines on the use of other trade-related government interventions, and the institutional arrangements for monitoring and enforcing compliance with those disciplines. It is progress in these latter three areas that determines the security of increases in market access from reductions in tariffs and the elimination of quantitative restrictions. Since the gains from trade liberalisation depend heavily on the stimulus it provides to trade-related investment, the security aspect is crucial.

Agricultural Products: Increased market access for agricultural products includes the "tariffication" of all non-tariff border measures (conversion to tariff-equivalents)—with the exception of those products for which special treatment has been negotiated—and a binding of all tariffs on agricultural products. As a result, the security of trade in agricultural products will for the first time be greater than in industrial products, since 100 per cent of agricultural product tariff lines will be bound.

Tariffs resulting from the "tariffication" process, together with the other tariffs on agricultural products, are to be reduced by a simple average of 36 per cent over six years in the case of developed countries and 24 per cent over ten years in the case of developing countries, with minimum reductions per tariff line of 15 per cent and 10 per cent, respectively. The reductions in the tariffs of developed countries—which account for about two-thirds of world imports of agricultural products—indicate an average percentage reduction of 37 per cent. With respect to individual product categories, developed countries will cut tariffs by above-average amounts on oilseeds, flowers and plants; and cut tariffs by below-average amounts on sugar and dairy products, with other product categories close to the average cut. In the categories of "topical products", which account for half of exports of developing countries of agricultural products, a 43 per cent reduction in tariffs will be implemented by developed countries.

Current access opportunities will be maintained on terms at least equivalent to those existing prior to the tariffication process. However, for those products where tariffication took place and imports were less than 5 per cent of domestic consumption because of the existing restrictions, minimum market access commitments, implemented through tariff quotas on an MFN basis at a low or minimal tariff rate, are required. Figures on the increased market access in terms of tonnage resulting from minimum access commitments indicate that substantial increases in market access occur for coarse grains (1,757,000 tons) and rice (1,076,000 tons), as well as for other products. With regard to commitments on export competition, the quantities of exports which can be legally subsidised must be reduced by 21 per cent. Furthermore, total export subsidy outlays will decline by 36 per cent, from $21.3 billion to $13.7 billion by the end of the transition period. The importance of this commitment is that, on average, developed countries subsidised annually during 1986-90 48.2 million tons of wheat, 19.5 million tons of coarse grains, 1.8 million tons of sugar, 1.2 million tons of beef, etc. With regard to commitments on domestic support to agricultural producers, total outlays (in terms of the Aggregate Measurement of Support) will be reduced by 18 per cent, from $197 billion to $162 billion by the end of the transition period.

The new market access opportunities for agricultural products which will result from the Uruguay Round—as a result of a change in border measures, and policies relating to export competition and domestic support—will be of particular interest to developing countries exporting temperature food products. More generally, multilateral discipliners on trade-distorting practices in agriculture are expected to stabilize world food markets in the coming decades, providing potential trade opportunities for developing countries and reducing fluctuations in food import bills, However, the potential situation in net food-importing developing countries is of particular concern. Potential problems relating to least-developed and net food importing developing countries are the subject of the Decision on *Measures Concerning the Possible Negative Effects of the Reform Programme on Least-Developed and Net Food Importing Developing Countries*. The Decision sets out objectives with regard to the provision of food aid, the provision of basic foodstuffs in full grant form and aid for agricultural development. It also refers to the possibility of assistance from the International Monetary Fund and the World Bank with respect to the short-term financing of food imports. The WTO Committee of Agriculture will monitor the implementation of the Decision.

WTO Agreements Covering Trade in Goods

GATT 1994: The cornerstone of trade relations in the area of goods. Differential and more favourable treatment to developing countries and to least-developed countries is permitted under the 1979 Enabling Clause with respect to tariffs in the context of the Generalised System of Preferences (GSP) and non-tariff measures, notwithstanding the most-favoured-nation clause, and with respect to regional or global arrangements concluded by developing countries.

Agreements Integrating Practices Otherwise on the Margin of GATT Rules: Includes trade-related investment measures (TRIMs) (which can be found to be inconsistent with the national treatment provision or the prohibition on quantitative restrictions), such as local content requirements or trade-balancing requirements. GATT inconsistent TRIMs are required to be notified and eliminated within a transition period of two years (developed countries), five years (developing countries) or seven years (least-developed countries). A further extension may be requested by developing and least-developed countries. The Agreement on Safeguards prohibits the use of "grey-area measures", such as voluntary restraints or orderly marketing arrangements; such measures are to be notified and eliminated.

Agreement on Textiles and Clothing: Provides for the eventual elimination of the Multi-Fibre Arrangement (MFA) after a ten-year transition period. In place since 1973, the MFA currently groups eight "importers"; of these, Austria, Canada, the European Communities, Finland, Norway and the United States apply restrictions under the MFA, while Japan and Switzerland do not. The other participants in the MFA are the "exporters" (mainly developing countries), whose exports or part of their exports covered by the MFA are subject to bilaterally agreed quantitative restraints or unilaterally imposed restraints on imports, typically applied at the product level but in some cases to various aggregates as wells.

Trade in Services

The General Agreement on Trade in Services (GATS) is the first multilateral agreement on trade that has its objective the progressive liberalisation of trade in services. It provide for secure and more open market in services in a similar manner as the GATT has done for trade in goods. The Agreement covers trade in all service sectors and the supply of service in all forms.

The GATS has two components: the framework agreement containing 29 Articles and a number of Annexes, Ministerial Decisions etc., as well as the schedules of commitments undertaken by each Member to bind the existing degree of openness or remove existing restrictions.

Of importance to developing countries is the fact that virtually all Member have made commitments on the movement of natural persons, even if these are circumscribed by the requirement of intra-corporate transferee status. In addition, commitments made by developed countries generally cover the cross-border supply of labour-intensive services such as computer-related services, professional and construction services. Further, most developing countries have committed themselves to bind or liberalize tourism and travel service, including, for example, the liberalisation of foreign investment restrictions for hotel and resort operators. These commitments are likely to improve the supply capacity of this key sector, which provides the major source of foreign exchange earnings in a number of island developing countries and least-developed countries. In addition, a number of developing countries have taken the opportunity the GATS provides to schedule commitments, thereby binding their own domestic reform process. Improvements in the quality of service that will result from liberalisation and increased competition will contribute to improved efficiency, consumer welfare and growth in developing countries as well as all other countries.

Intellectual Property Rights

Under the WTO, the number of countries providing intellectual property protection will increase over time. Developed countries have one year to meet their obligations, developing countries have five years and least developed countries have eleven years, with the possibility of an extension. Special transitional arrangements apply in the situation where a developing country does not presently provide patent protection in a particular chemical.

Adherence to the Paris and Berne Conventions is fairly widespread among developing countries. Many developing countries already providc minimum standards of intellectual property protection on a national treatment basis, although the scope of such protection varies significantly. Potential benefits for developing countries emerging from the Uruguay Round include a framework more conducive to domestic research efforts and to technology transfer and foreign direct investment. There will, however, be additional administrative burdens of enforcing such rights (specifically dealt with under the TRIPS Agreement), potentially higher royalty payments and adjustment costs for industries which, in the absence of domestic legislation in the areas, were producing goods that would be considered as counterfeit in the future. These will also be requirements relating to patents which may well mean an increase in prices of certain goods in some developing countries. Pharmaceutical and agricultural products present examples. These increases are expected to be small, and there are provisions in the Agreement itself to minimize any adverse implications for developing countries.

Dispute Settlement

From the perspective of developing countries, it should be noted that the elements of the 1966 Decision on Dispute

Settlement will continue to apply under the WTO dispute settlement procedures. Although this Decision has seldom been used, mainly because developing countries have only recently become more frequent users of the GATT dispute settlement procedures, it contains features of specific interest to developing countries, including automatic access to the "good offices" of the Director-General of the GATT/WTO to mediate and seek to find a satisfactory resolution to the dispute, and shorter time-limits in which panels must complete their deliberations.

Monitoring of Trade Policies

The TPRM provide for a Trade Policies Review Body to examine regularly the trade policies and practices of Members, every two years for the four major traders (the EU, US, Japan and Canada), every four years for the next sixteen leading traders, and every six years for the remaining traders, although longer intervals may be prescribed for least-developed countries.

The TPR process has helped countries assess their trade and economic reforms, and may have contributed to some portion of the liberalisation that has taken place under the Uruguay Round. In the future, the TPR process will help WTO Members evaluate their implementation of the Agreements, as well as provide an early warning of trends of potential concern to all participants in the trading system.

5

The WTO Dispute Settlement Mechanism

The Uruguay Round's new dispute settlement mechanism represents the new teeth of the World Trade Organisation (WTO). "The dispute settlement system of the WTO is a central element in providing security and predictability to the multilateral trading system", states the Understanding on Rules and Procedures Governing the Settlement of Disputes.

In the Final Act, WTO members have committed themselves not to take unilateral action against perceived violations of the trade rules. Instead, they have pledged to seek recourse in the new dispute-settlement system, and abide by its rules and procedures.

The Understanding emphasizes that prompt settlement of disputes is essential to the effective functioning of the WTO. Thus, it sets out in great detail the procedures and the timetable to be followed in resolving disputes—in contrast with the current GATT whose dispute-settlement provisions are contained in just two Articles. The existing GATT procedures have been built up over time through the evolution of customary practice, and later codified in decisions by GATT contracting parties—notably the 1979 Understanding and a provisional streamlining of the system in the 1989 Improvements following the Mid-Term Review of the Round.

Under the WTO, there will be one *Dispute Settlement Body(DSB)* dealing with disputes arising from any agreement contained in the Final Act. Thus, the DSB will have the sole authority to establish panels, adopt panel and appellate reports, maintain surveillance of implementation of rulings and recommendations, and authorize retaliatory measures in cases of non-implementation of recommendations. This is a significant improvement over the current GATT, under which dispute settlement is fragmented between the Council and the various Tokyo Round Committees.

Other important new features distinguish the WTO mechanism from that of GATT. In the WTO, there has to be a consensus against the establishment of panels or adoption of panel reports for these decisions not to be made whereas the reverse is true for the current system. Thus, parties to the dispute in the new system can no longer block these decisions. Another new feature is the possibility of appealing panel decisions to a standing Appellate Body. And, in line with the new integrated nature of the WTO mechanism, complainants, as a last resort, may take retaliatory action—suspend concessions—under an agreement different from the one covering the dispute against a member that has not implemented adopted panel recommendations.

The following are the various stages involved in setting disputes in the WTO:

Consultations

The aim of the WTO dispute-settlement mechanism is "to secure a positive solution to a dispute". Thus, developing a mutually acceptable solution consistent with WTO provisions to a problem between members is encouraged throughout the dispute-settlement process.

The first stage of settling disputes is the holding of consultations between the members concerned. Any member should reply promptly (within 10 days) to a request for consultations, and enter into consultations within 30 days from the date of the request. To ensure transparency, any request for consultations should be notified to the DSB in writing, providing the reasons for the request, including identification of the measure at issue and the legal basis for the complaint.

If consultations fail, and if both parties so agree, the case at this stage can be brought to the WTO Director-General, who, acting in an ex-officio capacity, will be ready to offer good offices, conciliation or mediation to settle the dispute.

Establishment of Panels

If the member concerned do not respond to a request for consultations within 10 days or if the consultations fail to arrive at a solution after 60 days, the complainant can ask the DSB to establish a panel to examine the case.

The establishment of a panel is almost automatic. The procedures require that the DSB should establish a panel no later than the second time it considers the panel request, unless there is a consensus against the decision. This means that the government which is the subject of the complaint cannot block the establishment of the panel.

The determination of the panel's terms of reference as well as its composition is also straightforward. The understanding provides for standard terms of reference that mandate the panel to examine the complaint in the light of the agreement cited, and to make findings that will assist the DSB in making recommendations or in giving rulings provided for in that agreement. The panel may operate under different terms of reference, if the parties concerned so agree.

The panel is to be constituted within 30 days of its establishment. The WTO Secretariat will suggest the names of three potential panellists to the parties to the dispute, drawing as necessary on a list of qualified persons (including, for example, those who have previously participated in panel proceedings, or have been representatives to GATT, or have taught international trade law). If the parties cannot agree on the panellists within 20 days from the establishment of the panel, at the request of either party, the Director General, in consultations with the DSB Chairman and the Chairman of the relevant Committee or Council, will appoint the panellists. The panellists will serve in their individual capacities and will not be subjects to government instructions.

Panel Procedures

The understanding provides that the period in which the panel conducts its examination of the case—that is, from the time the terms of reference and composition of the panel are agreed to the time the panel's final report is given to the parties to the dispute—should not exceed six months. In cases of urgency, including those relating to perishable goods, the timeframe is shortened to three months. In no case should the period from the establishment of the panel to the circulation of the report to the Members exceed nine months.

Detailed working procedures for the panel are set out in the Understanding (see chart on page 32).

Adoption of Panel Reports

The WTO procedures provide that a panel report is to be adopted by the DSB within 60 days of issuance, unless one party notifies its decision to appeal or a consensus emerges against the adoption of the report.

The DSB cannot consider the adoption of a panel report earlier than 20 days after it has been circulated to members. Members which have objections to the report are required to state their reasons in writing, for circulation before the DSB meeting at which the panel report will be considered.

Appellate Review

A new feature of the WTO dispute settlement mechanism gives the possibility of appeal to either party in

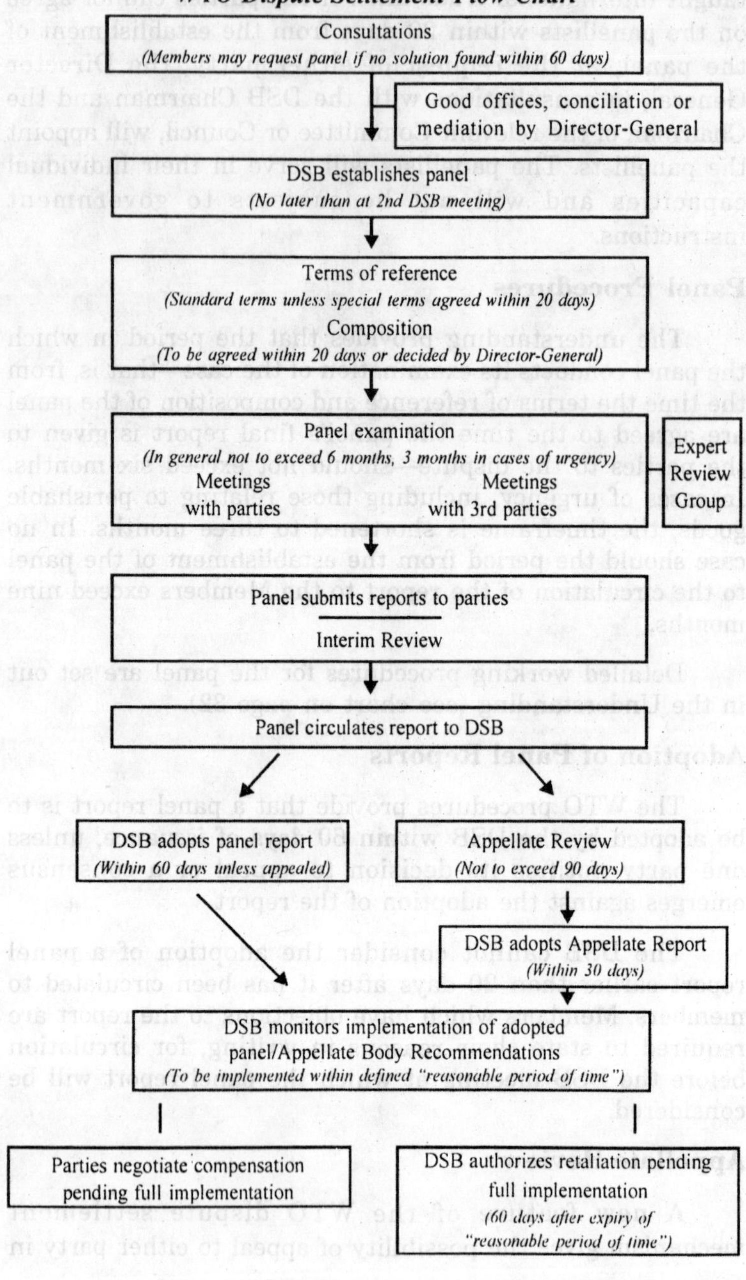
WTO Dispute Settlement Flow Chart
Consultations
(Members may request panel if no solution found within 60 days)
Good offices, conciliation or mediation by Director-General
DSB establishes panel
(No later than at 2nd DSB meeting)
Terms of reference
(Standard terms unless special terms agreed within 20 days)
Composition
(To be agreed within 20 days or decided by Director-General)
Panel examination
(In general not to exceed 6 months, 3 months in cases of urgency)
Meetings with parties
Meetings with 3rd parties
Expert Review Group
Panel submits reports to parties
Interim Review
Panel circulates report to DSB
DSB adopts panel report
(Within 60 days unless appealed)
Appellate Review
(Not to exceed 90 days)
DSB adopts Appellate Report
(Within 30 days)
DSB monitors implementation of adopted panel/Appellate Body Recommendations
(To be implemented within defined "reasonable period of time")
Parties negotiate compensation pending full implementation
DSB authorizes retaliation pending full implementation
(60 days after expiry of "reasonable period of time")

a panel proceeding. However, any appeal shall be limited to issues of law covered in the panel report and the legal interpretation developed by the panel.

All appeals will be heard by a standing Appellate Body to be established by the DSB. This Appellate Body will be composed of seven persons—broadly representative of the WTO membership—who will serve four-year terms. They are to be persons of recognised standing in the field of law and international trade, and not affiliated with any government.

Three members of the Appellate Body sit at any one time to hear appeals. They can uphold, modify or reverse the legal findings and conclusions of the panel. As a general rule, the appeal proceedings are not to exceed 60 days but in no case shall they exceed 90 days.

Thirty days after issuance, the Appellate Body report is to be adopted by the DSB and unconditionally accepted by the parties to the dispute—unless there is consensus against its adoption.

Implementation

The Understanding stresses that "prompt compliance with recommendations or rulings of the DSB is essential in order to ensure effective resolution of disputes to the benefit of all Members."

At a DSB meeting held within 30 days of the adoption of the panel or appellate report, the party concerned must state its intentions in respect of the implementation of the recommendations. If it is impractical to comply immediately, the member will be given a "reasonable period of time"—to be set by the DSB—to do so. If it fails to act within this period, it is obliged to enter into negotiations with the complainant in order to determine a mutually acceptable compensation.

If after 20 days, no satisfactory compensation is agreed, the complainant may request authorisation from the DSB to suspend concessions or obligations against the other party. The procedures provide that the DSB should grant this authorisation within 30 days of the expiry of the "reasonable period of time" unless there is a consensus against the request.

If the member concerned objects to the level of suspension, the matter will be referred to arbitration. This will be carried out by the original panel members, and if this is not possible, by an arbitrator appointed by the WTO Director General. Arbitration should be completed within 60 days of the expiry of the "reasonable period of time", and the resulting decision should be accepted by the parties concerned as final and not subject to another arbitration. The DSB, upon request, then authorizes the suspension of concessions consistent with the findings of the arbitrator, unless there is a consensus to reject the request.

In principle, concessions should be suspended in the same sector as that in issue in the panel case. If this is not practicable or effective, the suspension can be made in a different sector of the same agreement. In turn, if this is not effective or practicable and if the circumstances are serious enough, the suspension of concessions may be made under another agreement.

In any case, the DSB will keep under surveillance the implementation of adopted recommendations or rulings, and any outstanding case will remain on its agenda until the issue is resolved.

6

High World Trade Growth Vs. Output

WTO Sees Link to Globalisation

World trade in merchandise goods is expected to increase in volume by 8 per cent in 1995 down marginally on the very high 9½ per cent for 1994. Although the current outlook is for a further modest slowing next year, trade growth will remain above the average of the past decade.

Recent trade growth figures continue to exceed world production growth by a large margin in 1995 probably by a factor of almost three and next year close to double. This persistent pattern relates closely to the "globalisation" of the world economy; a process which, brings far-reaching benefits and which can be promoted through the further development of the multilateral trading system.

The recent growth is as follows:

- a 13 per cent rise pushed the value of world merchandise trade past the $4,000 billion mark for the first time, to $4,090 billion;
- an 8 per cent increase in the value of trade in commercial services, to $1,100 billion, after near stagnation in 1993;
- a 23 per cent increase in the dollar value of merchandise trade in the first six months of 1995 which, allowing for the depreciation of the US dollar, is consistent with a full-year growth in trade volume of 8 per cent.

Globalisation

Over the period from 1950 (when the process of trade liberalisation through the early GATT Round got under-way) to 1994, the volume of world merchandise trade increased at an annual rate of slightly more than 6 per cent and world output by close to 4 per cent. Thus, during those 45 years world merchandise trade multiplied 14 times and output 5½ times. However, the excess of trade growth over output growth varied; from an average of a mere half percentage point in the period 1974-84 to nearly 3½ percentage points in the most recent 10 years. In fact, the excess during the years since 1990 has been much higher still but it is not yet clear whether or not this represents a permanent shift to a faster rate of increase in the world's trade-to-output ratio.

To the question "will globalisation continue?" In this regard one has to observe two factors—technological change and the evolving strategies of firms and individual investors—impart a natural momentum to global integration. It is government policies which can speed-up, slow down or even reverse progress on global integration. In this context, the role of non-discrimination—in particular, through the "most-favoured-nation" (MFN) clause—is examined.

The MFN Clause

MFN was the centrepiece of a multiplicity of bilateral trade agreements reached in Europe in the second half of the 19th century, a period marked by very low tariffs and rapidly increasing trade. In contrast, the 1920s and the 1930s saw efforts to restore liberal trade through international trade conferences rather than legally-binding commercial treaties based on MFN. The failure of these efforts contributed to the Great Depression and provided some of the roots of military confrontation in 1939. It was only after the War that negotiations established what became the GATT, a multilateral contract consisting of rules and disciplines and based firmly (Article) on MFN treatment.

The GATT system has been a post-war bulwark against a return to the trade chaos of the 1930's. In the 1990's, a disintegration of the globalised international economy on the scale of 1930's is almost unthinkable. In contrast, today "the threat that would be posed by a loss of credibility of the multilateral rules" (now represented by the WTO) would be "a fracturing of the global economy into inward-looking and potentially antagonistic trading blocs".

One can suggest two safeguards against such an eventuality:

- the examination of new ways to ensure that free-trade areas and customs unions remain outward-looking and complement rather than compete with the multilateral trading system; and
- progress in dealing, at the multilateral level, with new issues tied directly to the further evolution of the global economy. These include telecommunications, financial services, environment, competition and investment policies among others.

Progress in dealing with these and other issues at the multilateral level will have a significant impact on the future pace of global integration, both directly and through its impact on the credibility of the multilateral system in influencing the broad spectrum of national trade policies.

7

The Trade-related Intellectual Property Rights (TRIPS) Agreement and the Developing Countries

The basic norms of free competition established in the nineteenth century induced legislators to provide relatively weak forms of intellectual property protection. Often innovators could rely only on such factors as lead time, reputation for quality and continuing technical improvements to maintain their foothold in the market.

Undermining this outlook were two developments that led to the inclusion of intellectual property issues in the World Trade Organisation (WTO). First, the rise of knowledge-based industries radically altered the nature of competition and disrupted the equilibrium that had resulted from more traditional comparative advantages. Second, the growing capacity of manufacturers in developing countries to penetrate distant markets for traditional industrial products forced the developed countries to rely more heavily on their comparative advantages in the production of intellectual goods than in the past. Market access for developing countries thus became a bargaining chip to be exchanged for greater protection of intellectual goods within a restructured global market place.

Since 1986 the developed countries' drive for extraterritorial protection of intellectual property rights has largely ignored the competitive capabilities of developing countries with respect to intellectual goods, and it has also downplayed these countries' rights to preferential treatment under existing rules. At the same time, the logic of multilateral trade negotiations skews the pre-existing North-South conflict over intellectual property rights by introducing the prospects of trade concessions in unrelated fields. Intellectual property rights constitute but one of many variables that bear on competitive capacity and the transfer of technology in general.

Primary Intellectual Property Regimes

Patents

The extension of patentability to virtually all types of technology recognised by developed patent systems, the prolongation of patent protection to a uniform term of twenty years, and legal recognition of the patentee's exclusive rights to import the relevant products could adversely affect developing countries whose existing patent laws fall below these standards. In practice, however, the competitive status of any given developing country in a post-TRIPS world will depend in part on the level of foreign direct investment it attracts and on the benefits that strengthened intellectual property rights bring to domestic innovators.

Competition under stronger patent regimes requires developing countries to adopt legal means of narrowing the scope of foreign patent monopolies and of encouraging local entrepreneurs either to work around the claimed inventions or to develop improvements suited to local conditions. To this end, local entrepreneurs should exploit technical information in disclosures published abroad; patent authorities should exercise all of the claims limitations practised abroad; and domestic courts should strictly interpret the doctrine of equivalents. Legislative enactment of utility model laws would provide additional incentives to adapt foreign inventions to local conditions and to improve them further.

Moreover, unpatented traditional technologies will often remain suitable for local needs, and the resulting products may be sold at lower prices than imported products of patented technologies. Entrepreneurs in developing countries should also be prepared to exploit unpatented applications of applied scientific know-how in such advanced technologies as biogenetic engineering and computer programme-related innovation.

In time, increased direct investment by foreign patentees could enable developing-country licensees who exploit their natural advantages, especially low labour costs, to succeed on both domestic and export markets where non-licensees were unable or unwilling to venture in the past. Familiarisation with the benefits of the patent system should stimulate greater investment in domestic research and development and in technological innovation.

The gradual extension of patents to new technologies such as computer programmes and bio-genetic engineering without the emergence of agreed international minimum standards creates both opportunities and risks for the developing countries. While the developed countries enjoy unique advantages in biotechnology that only become available to developing countries as a consequence of stronger patent systems, some developing countries may find their own competitive status enhanced by the provision of proprietary rights, including plant breeders' rights, though others may not. The patenting of biogenetic advances decreases the scope for reverse-engineering and could also increase the costs of doing business in key sectors of some developing economies, notably agriculture. As regards information technologies, reliance on copyright and trade secrets at the international level appears less unfavourable to the developing countries' prospects than patents, for reasons that are set out below. However, the tendency to patent software could diminish these prospects by posing limits to reverse engineering and to the attainment of the interoperability, and this trend adds to the overall costs of disseminating information goods.

To the extent that patented technology is not made available on reasonable terms or that un-wholesome economic dependencies actually arise, developing countries will have to consider measures to restore the competitive balance that are consistent with the TRIPS Agreement. For example, the agreement allows compulsory licences when the rights holders fail to licences patented technology "on reasonable commercial terms". It also provides other bases for defensive regulatory action by emphasizing "the transfer and dissemination of technology, to the mutual advantage of producers and users" and the need "to promote the public interest in sectors of vital importance to socio-economic and technological development".

Measures to restrain abuse of intellectual property rights as authorised by the Paris Convention also remain available under the TRIPS agreement, which expressly empowers developing countries to deal with licensing practices that "adversely affect the international transfer of technology".

Finally, the agreement specifically preserves the right of all states to "adopt measures necessary to protect public health and nutrition and to promote the public interest in sectors of vital importance to socio-economic and technological development, provided that such measures are consistent with the provisions of this agreement".

Trade-marks and Geographical Indications

The TRIPS provisions give pre-existing norms greater specificity while softening the use requirement and eliminating both compulsory licences and local linkage requirements. These provisions also subject the international regime of trade-marks and unfair competition to more stringent enforcement measures, including border controls against imports of counterfeit goods.

As a result, developing countries will need to reassess the pro-competitive functions of trade marks in open economies while addressing questions of abuse in a more direct fashion. They should insist on receiving the technical cooperation and aid that the TRIPS agreement envisages for the purpose of defraying administrative and enforcement burdens.

Governments should consider policies and incentives that encourage enterprises to establish their own market identities through appropriate trade-marks and foreign firms to allow licensees to adopt more of the licenced products for both domestic and export needs under local trade-marks.

Copyrights

Authors in many developing countries are very active in both domestic and foreign markets. It nonetheless remains true that the balance of trade in cultural goods favours exports from developed countries. This imbalance could increase under the TRIPS agreement, which generally applies the international minimum standards of the Berne Convention, plus selected standards from the Rome Convention on neighbouring rights.

While efforts to implement these standards is mandatory, developing-country authorities should familiarize themselves with the extent to which the scope of copyright protection varies from country to country, in the absence of authoritative legal limitations recognised by international law. Carefully framed public-interest exceptions may further reduce the overall costs of a TRIPS Agreement without violating international copyright norms. Moreover, the revised Berne Convention already provides for compulsory licences for educational and scientific test, and developing countries may wish to consider making greater use of these concessions.

Ancillary Proprietary Regimes

Trade Secrets

In modern economies trade secret law regulates the pace of competition by endowing second comers with an absolute right to reverse-engineer. To operate successfully under such a regime, developing countries must realign the concept of "transfer of technology" with the nature of competition on open markets. Technology is transferred through self-help methods of reverse engineering. The potential benefits of reverse-engineering unpatented technologies increase when advanced technologies are involved, notably biogenetic engineering, computer programmes and computer-aided design. The unpatented, non-copyrightable know-how underlying these technologies is often embodied in tangible products available to the public, which renders classical trade secret protection of doubtful efficacy. By ignoring this problem, the TRIPS Agreement provides entrepreneurs in developing countries with major opportunities, notwithstanding the extension of trade secret law under TRIPS, provided they are willing and able to master the art of reverse-engineering.

Other Proprietary Regimes

The TRIPS Agreement mandates intellectual property protection for industrial designs, plant varieties and integrated circuit designs. Although the developed countries enjoy a clear advantage in advanced sectors of industrial design, more traditional sectors rooted in aesthetic appeal rather than technical efficiency remain accessible to firms in developing countries.

Need for Multilateral Policies

Global economic integration increasingly requires that intangible creations receive minimum international standards of legal protection. Purely territorial intellectual property rights will thus give way to international sovereignty. However, the norms of that law represent a delicate balance between the interests of States at different stages of development, so that the evolution of international intellectual property law will have to accommodate these norms and that balance.

Efforts to implement higher intellectual property standards will put increasing strains on competition law, which is not directly covered by the TRIPS Agreement. Identifying the parameters of healthy competition valid for all players in an integrated world market will become a pressing task for the international community in a post-TRIPS world. These issues will be complicated by the fact that innovators, users and second comers all have different stakes in fashioning the rules of unfair competition law, and their interests will increasingly vary more with their economic roles than with the geopolitical affiliations of their respective national States.

Competition law must, become an integral part of international discussions of intellectual property rights, and there is a great need for multilateral cooperation to achieve a marketwide balance between incentives to create, and reasonable opportunities to imitate and improve upon, technological innovation. These discussions should lead to an internationally agreed framework for promoting a transfer of technology that is compatible with the drive for greater economic efficiency. To the extent that such cooperation succeeds, it will contribute a new perspective to the notion of fair competition that should strengthen the prospects of all participants in the global marketplace.

8

New Agenda of the WTO

One "new" issue that is already in the WTO work programme is the relationship between trade and the environment. At the heart of the matter is how to relate the rules-based multilateral trade system, continued trade liberalisation and further development of the global economy to environmental concerns and objectives. It is possible to envisage circumstances in which trade, unsupported by sound environmental policy, could involve damage to the environment—or, on the contrary, in which environmental regulations could harm legitimate trade. In such circumstances, however, careful judgment is necessary in weighing whether it is trade policy or environmental policy which must be adjusted, it is also not difficult to see how ill-considered international environmental agreement could needlessly frustrate trade and reduce incomes and even put risk environmental reform and improvement. At the same time, it is just as important to recognize the circumstances in which, by encouraging efficiency and a better allocation of scarce resources, trade liberalisation may be supportive of an improved environment. The WTO will contribute to a better understanding of the issues, and assist governments in developing more coherent polices in this area.

Trade and investment is leading candidate for the new agenda, since one of the consequences of globalisation is to lessen the distinctions among different forms of market access. In the GATT framework, market access simply in terms of tariffs and non-tariff measures. Reducing tariffs and eliminating other trade barriers at the frontier was the recipe for liberalisation. Foreign investment was an altogether different matter. Indeed, countries often used to regard tariffs and other trade barriers as convenient mechanisms for inducing foreign investment. Protection of the domestic market offered attractive profits to foreign investors. This was the essence of the import substitution development strategy—a strategy that in large measure failed and has now been discredited. In today's world of international business, trade and investment are increasingly viewed as complements, not substitutes. Different parts of internationally-based businesses can be located in several different countries. Increasingly, businesses trade to invest, and invest to trade. The WTO cannot afford to concern itself only with the trade side of the equation—that would be to deny the reality of modern global business practices.

It is not coincidence that foreign direct investment flows worldwide quadrupled, to almost US $200 billion per annum, in the ten years to 1993. Indeed, the importance of investment was recognised in the General Agreement on Trade in Services negotiated in the Uruguay Round, where investment, or commercial presence, was one of the four modes of service supply in respect of which WTO members undertook market access commitments. But there is a need for a broader, or more horizontal approach to international investment rules. Such rules would build on the WTO principles of non-discrimination and national treatment, and create a policy environment to encourage and safeguard foreign investment, whether in goods or services.

Governments will increasingly recognize the need for work on investment in a more global setting as well. Especially so since developing countries are not only the target of a growing proportion of international investment but are themselves becoming important overseas investors. One should note that the Uruguay Round Agreement on Trade-related Investment Measures calls for an examination by members within five years of the case for developing provisions on investment policy.

That same mandate refers to competition policy, which also has to be examined as a possible candidate for further work. Of course, what has done in the GATT and the WTO over 50 years in promoting a liberal trading environment is precisely the enhancement of competition. But if we have succeeded in getting the rules of competition between countries to work effectively, that very success requires us to go further and consider how the behaviour of companies can serve to distort international competition. The need to see whether there are any areas where explicit competition rules, or specific understandings, are necessary internationally to complement the statutes that many governments already have on their books. There is no doubt that competition rules are essential to the proper functioning of markets—the need to clarify, however, is how best to promote such disciplines, both nationally and internationally.

Trade and Social Standards: This is a highly controversial issue, and in the absence of a consensus there is no possibility that it could be brought into the agenda of the WTO. It is clear that what the need first and foremost is a comprehensive effort to bring some clarity to the many complex issues that are involved here.

The first issue to be clarified is the nature of the subject; talking about the comparative advantage of developing countries which comes from lower wage level—as the issue is sometimes presented—or talking about human rights or labour standard? It is fundamentally important to clarify the terms of the debate as it relates to trade. The second point is to identify what are the key issues related to trade; for example, talking about child labour or trade union rights in terms of labour standards or in terms of human rights? There are just some of the preconditions for opening a discussion on whether a useful debate is, in fact, possible on these issues. One of these principles is that economic and social growth and development are to a large extent interdependent. When the economic situation is poor, the social situation is also likely to be poor. And correspondingly, where there is economic growth, social development is more likely to come too.

While no-one should challenge the legitimate right of developing countries to use the comparative advantage of lower costs, and no-one should use human rights and issues of social standards as an excuse for disguised protectionism, no country should deliberately deny workers' rights or attempt to generate artificially-lower costs by forced labour, discrimination against women, exploitation of children or other such abuses.

No one should on no account allow this debate to re-open a North-South divide. Dialogue is the best approach to finding ways to improve the observance of labour standards. In order to convince developing countries that no protectionist considerations are involved in the debate, it is essential to prove that all possible measures other than trade sanctions are being taken to alleviate the problems. One excellent example is the Memorandum of Understanding on the elimination of child labour from the garments industry in Bangladesh that was signed in July 1995 by the industry, the ILO and UNICEF, with support from the Bangladesh and US Governments. This joint approach combines restrictions on child labour with the improvement of educational opportunities for the children involved. This is a targeted and constructive approach to a specific problem, and as such it offers a useful model for future efforts. On the other hand, to simply restrict imports of garments from the industries concerned would in all likelihood have just worsened the situation of these children.

Reciprocity and Regionalism

Reciprocity and the growth of regionalism in international trade relations is very important. There are from to time calls for trade policies based on reciprocity instead of the basic "Most Favoured Nations" (MFN) principle. These are based on the assumption that the degree of liberalisation already reached by certain countries does not give them any real defence in a multilateral negotiation vis-à-vis those countries whose liberalisation process is much less advanced. Advocates of reciprocity argue that such countries have no real incentive to deeper liberalisation, given their benefits from the MFN system.

To present reciprocity as an alternative to MFN is a major departure from the trading system built up over 50 years, and it is just the opposite of what the founding fathers of the multilateral system envisaged. A nation or regional group which believes itself to be an open market has the right to fight hard to obtain from all its partners the greatest possible degree of liberalisation. If this argument is used tactically and temporarily as a negotiating device, there is less need for alarm over its implications for the system as a whole. But if it becomes a permanent instrument of policy, then the risk for the multilateral system could become serious.

Trade is technical in its substance but highly political in its consequences. Reciprocity as a structural alternative to the multilateral system equals bilateralism; bilateralism equals discrimination; and trade relations based on power rather than rules are the result. This would be a very dangerous departure from the success story of the multilateral system.

The growth of regionalism is a more complex issue. There is no natural contradiction between regionalism and the multilateral system. This has been the shared assessment of the great majority of the international trade community. The real contradiction, it must always be emphasised, is between open trade and protectionism. Regional trade initiatives can certainly help to lower trade barriers and thus promote economic growth. But the relationship between regionalism and a multilateral system based on the MFN principle is nonetheless a complex one. The provisions of the GATT have sought to ensure compatibility by requiring regional agreements to cover substantially all trade among the partners and to promoted trade policies which do no lead to higher protection or extra restrictions on the trade of non-members. In practice, however, it has been almost impossible to assess the consistency of regional agreements.

The relation between regional and multilateral liberalisation in practice has been a different and generally more positive story. For example, successive enlargements of the European Union have been followed by multilateral trade negotiations, which have maintained a *de facto* link between progress at the regional level and at the multilatcral level. These links are the reason why most people have seen regional agreements as building blocks for multilateral free trade.

Until quite recently, there was only one large regional grouping, and that was limited to a number of western European countries. The US was historically opposed to regionalism. But this situation has changed since the 1980s, the US has begun to build its own regional agreements, though free trade with Canada, through NAFTA, and through APEC, etc. Now, almost all the member countries of the WTO also belong to a regional trade agreement. The importance of regional agreements as a means of tariff reduction has declined (this is also thanks to the success of the GATT). Regional agreements are becoming more and more important in terms of trade rules, and for the political weight they represent in international negotiations. These are elements which could break up the parallelism between regional and multilateral progress; there is the risk that antagonism between regional groups could make progress in the multilateral system more difficult.

Furthermore, regional initiatives such as the suggestions for a trans-Atlantic free trade area could give the impression of re-erecting a discriminatory divide between the rich North and the poorer South. One must be very attentive to strengthening the linkage which has existed up to now between regional and multilateral progress. What this means in practical terms is that regional liberalisation initiatives must proceed almost in tandem with multilateral ones. What countries are willing to do regionally, they must then be willing to do multilaterally, so as to keep this parallelism between regional and multilateral commitments.

At the core of this relationship, there is the basic question of the kind of international system, that is needed a global system based on the principle of non-discrimination embodied in agreed and enforceable rules, or a world divided into regional blocs with all the consequences this would imply for political stability and security.

An Unusual Historic Opportunity

To sum up, it is clear that the challenges facing the multilateral trading system are about much more than trade matters as they used to be defined. For some people—and for some countries too—the pace of change is unsettling and even alarming. Whether in the challenges that the information revolution presents to anyone over 30, or in the pace of economic globalisation, there is an understandable reflex which asks the world to slow down a little. However, we know it will not.

That is why there is a need to keep the multilateral system, with its reliable framework of principles and rules in good repair; it is a firm foothold in a shifting world. Liberalisation within the multilateral system means that this unstoppable process can be implemented within internationally agreed rules and disciplines. This is the opposite of a chaotic and unchecked process—without the security of the multilateral system, change would indeed be a leap in the dark.

At the same time, the multilateral system is becoming more and more a political issue. This is happening because its evolution increasingly concerns national regulatory policies more than cross-border obstacles, and it is happening because the challenges to the system are increasingly political rather than technical. In this context, it could become very important to consider the possibility of strengthening the institutional basis of the system, for example by enhancing the political dimension of its central institution, the WTO.

The confluence of political and economic events of the last few years places everyone on the threshold of an unusual historic opportunity: that of establishing a truly global system for the conduct of international economic relations, a system that responds readily to change and to changing needs, and one for which every nation will wish to claim ownership.

9

Winners and Lossers

The WTO and the Developing Countries

The World Trade Organisation (WTO) began work on January 1, 1995. The new international body's tasks include implementing the results of the Uruguay Round, which reach far beyond the old General Agreement of Tariffs and Trade (GATT). Besides the traditional GATT remit of overseeing trade in goods, the results of the eighth round of GATT talks encompass among other things rules on trade in services, protecting intellectual property, and wider institutional competences in settling trade disputes. Furthermore, GATT's old no-go areas such as trade in agro-products textiles and clothing, were integrated in its body of rules.

The role and participation of developing countries underwent considerable changes during the course of the new Uruguay Round. Before the talks began, many governments of the South took a highly critical stance on the taking up of the negotiations, and above all on the widening of their brief. Leading critics among the developing countries, such as Brazil and India, called for the effective implementation of the results of the Tokyo round (1973-79) before beginning new talks. This thumbs-down gave a glimpse once again of the unity of developing countries, which during the 1970s set the trade policy agenda and contributed to the flourishing of the UN Conference on Trade and Development (UNCTAD). But their increasing differences in economic interests were soon reflected in disparate negotiating positions during the GATT talks. In some sectors such as agricultural trade, the developing countries no longer had any common interests whatsoever. Nevertheless, both during and after the round there were various attempts to assess the possible impacts of trade liberalisation on the developing countries as a whole. The World Bank and the OECD's Development Assistance Committee tried very early in the negotiations to make the possible results palatable for the developing countries with encouraging projections. The developing countries' high rate of accession to the WTO reflects the growing importance of the world trade order for them. And many of them are meanwhile pushing ahead with liberalisation of their own economies, partly of their own accord and partly in the context of structural adjustment programmes. But they often evaluate the results of the Uruguay Round quite differently. The following is aimed at summarizing briefly the possible political and economic impacts of the developing countries, which have been the subject of debate so far.

Stricter Rules on World Trade

The Uruguay Round led to a widening and strengthening of the body of rules on world trade. Its widening covered the inclusion of the above-mentioned new sectors and the old areas of exception. Its strengthening relates to the drawing up of stricter rules for fixing standards to counter the growing use of non-tariff obstacles to trade, and to the new procedure for settling disputes. While under the old rules all treaty states had to approve the ruling of an arbitration procedure—including the "loser" country—to make it valid, an arbitration now takes effect directly. Only its unanimous rejection by the treaty signatories can make it null and void.

NGOs in the North and the South in particular interpret both the widening and strengthening critically. In their view, the changes give the WTO too much power. They fear that national political decisions in future could be assessed and attacked as possible trade obstacles. They say this reduces the already limited possibilities of nation states to determine important policy fields, such as the environment and social or regional policy.

Strong and Weak Members

However, to what extent these legal remedies can actually be resorted to in the everyday life of global trade policy remains to be seen in the near future. As early as during US ratification of the Uruguay Round, the Clinton Administration commented that if USA were to be censured three times by a GATT dispute process it would reserve the right to leave the organisation again. Since weaker trade partners lack the possibility to take pain-inflicting counter measures, the different trade policy weights of the WTO members will also count in future practice.

The estimates of individual groups of developing countries on possible economic profits stemming from Uruguay Round differ greatly. Projections of potential trade profits were downright euphoric even before the end of the negotiations.

The general reduction of customs duties on industrial goods—put about 37 per cent—will impact on the developing countries as a whole because the previous preferential tariffs will become relatively less important. There will be few changes for countries that have so far hardly taken advantage of preferences. But the cutback will impact in particular on African countries, which have the most extensive preferences, as well as on the ASEAN group, which were especially high users of the Generalised System of Preferences. A loss of 1.5 per cent is projected for Sub-Saharan Africa and the ACP states, and 1.9 per cent for LDC's. According to Overseas Development Institute (ODI) estimates, the figures for individual countries could be much worse. Ethiopia, Malawi, Mozambique and Guayana are likely to lose between 4.6 per cent and 5.9 per cent of their export earings.

Agricultural Markets Remain Distorted

In the agricultural sector, the net food importers among the developing countries will be losers because they will have to pay moderately higher prices for their imports. The forecasts of losses, however, are not so high since no far-reaching liberalisation can be achieved in the agro-sector. The two main adversaries in Uruguay Round's dispute over agriculture, the USA and the EU, were able in the Blair House Agreement to reach an accord on only a very limited reduction of their high support payments to their farmers. Even cutbacks in export subsidies were pegged at about only 21 per cent in volume and about 36 per cent in value. That is why export subsidies will continue to exert pressure on world market prices. At the same time, the slight reduction will mean the net agricultural produce exporters among the developing countries will derive only marginal profit from the liberalisation.

On the positive side, the most important sector of projected profits for developing countries is textiles and clothing. The accord on these goods foresees the previous Multifibre Agreement (MFA) expiring within 10 years and textiles and clothing coming step-by-step under GATT rules. But it remains to be seen if that target can be achieved in that period, and how often in future the industrial countries will invoke the protective clause covering this sector to safeguard their own industries.

Weak States will Lose

Taking an overall look at the results of the Uruguay Round, it can be noted that those developing countries, which are strong in exports of industrial goods and have so far hardly used the Generalised System of Preferences, will profit economically. The losers will be countries, which will suffer from the erosion of the importance of preferences. Tottoing up, negative impacts of more than US $2 billion are forecast for Africa. Various sides—NGOs as well as some governments—are therefore now calling for compensation payments for net losers.

The developing countries lost unity came to life again towards the end of the Uruguay Round when new subjects for world trade order were put on the agenda. Some governments and NGOs are increasingly addressing the ecological and social impacts of the liberalisation of world trade. There are above all highly vocal in expressing fears that the globalisation of the world economy will be accompanied by a loss of national sovereignty over political measures in sectors such as the environment and social and regional policy. And that linked with an increasingly competitive situation in an ever more open world market. This will in the long-term have negative impacts on a country's ability to assert justified measures to protect its interests. The governments of most developing countries have clearly rejected these new proposals for discussion. They fear this bid could make the industrial nations' hopes for economic protectionism reappear.

New Role for WTO

There is no simple answer to these new agendas. Indeed, it is questionable if the WTO is a suitable forum to negotiate on them in detail. However, so long as a relatively effective government body on world trade relations has no counterpart in comparably effective instruments to deal with the social and ecological impacts of globalisation, there will probably be repeated attempts to assign new competencies to the WTO. Even when it would make more sense not to leave multilateral rules on environmental protection or securing human rights to a trade organisation. That nothing should block the objectives of sustainable development or safeguarding human rights, which go beyond trade policy, must thereby be beyond doubt.

10

Developing Countries and the Uruguay Round

An Evaluation and Prospects for the Future

The Uruguay Round was the most ambitious trade negotiation in history. It covered a wide variety of subjects relating to trade in goods; it brought under the aegis of multilateral disciplines two new sectors—agriculture and textiles—which had previously been exempt from such disciplines; it established new rules for services and intellectual property; and it set up a new World Trade Organisation (WTO) charged with supervising the results of the Round and continuing negotiations on all trade-related questions.

This article focuses on key issues of interest to developing countries. They are: (a) market access for developing country exports; (b) new restrictions on trade and industrial policy formulation in developing countries; (c) the effectiveness of the new safeguards and anti-dumping mechanisms in deterring protectionism; (d) the protection of intellectual property rights; (e) services; (f) the status of the principle of special and differential (S & D) treatment; and (g) institutional reforms and the creation of the WTO. An evaluation of the Round from the point of view of developing countries must necessarily attempt to weigh all of these elements.

The results of the Uruguay Round do not represent a good deal for developing countries. As regards improved market access for developing country exports, tariffs on products of interest to developing countries have been cut, but they will remain at higher levels than those applied to products traded mainly among developed countries; moreover, tariff escalation will be reduced but not significantly. The Round will bring about only marginal improvements in market access in the crucial areas of agriculture and textiles. Developing countries should continue to fight for the removal of tariffs on those goods that are of export interest to them and for the elimination of tariff escalation.

Market access will also depend on the abolition of grey area measures, their replacement by transparent and clearly temporary safeguard provisions, and the disciplining of antidumping practices. The new safeguards mechanism agreed to in the Round is due to replace grey area measures. However, the agreement legitimizes quantitative restrictions (QRS) directed at individual exporters, albeit with fairly stringent limitations as to duration and proof of injury procedures. Moreover, it remains to be seen in practice whether importers will resort to safeguards or will prefer the route of anti-dumping measures, which will remain easier to apply. Indeed, the anti-dumping agreement can be considered the major loophole of the Final Act and may well lead to a recrudescence of protectionism in both developed and—by imitation—developing countries.

The single most important achievement of the Uruguay Round was the setting up, under the aegis of the WTO, of an integrated and strengthened dispute settlement mechanism. While cross retaliation has been legitimised as a last resort, defendants will no longer be able to veto panel decisions that go against them. However, it is not yet clear to what extent the new dispute settlement mechanism will succeed in deterring major importers from having recourse to unilateral measures (such as those taken by the United States under the cover of Section 301 of its 1984 Trade Act).

As a result of the Round, there has been a significant upward harmonisation of trade and industrialisation policy disciplines towards the standards prevailing in developed countries. Henceforth, developing countries will face considerably more stringent restrictions in these areas, and their access to foreign technology will become more uncertain and costly. The Round has also resulted in a significant erosion in the international consensus in favour of special and differential (S & D) treatment for developing countries in the international trading system.

As the accords are implemented, developing countries will experience balance-of-payments difficulties. There will be a need to provide developing countries with greater International Monetary Fund (IMF) financing during the transition to the new disciplines, many of which will have adverse repercussions on the balance of payments of developing countries. Some of the agreements with balance-of-payments implications for developing countries are the adoption and enforcement of stricter intellectual property legislation, the agreement on agriculture, and the restrictions on the use of trade measures to protect the balance of payments.

The Final Act calls for cooperation between the WTO, the World Bank and the IMF. In the long-term, the main area of cooperation ought to be ensuring the consistency of international policies in the areas of trade, money and finance in order to ensure high rates of growth in the world economy and in developing countries in particular. It is especially important that such cooperation does not become an additional source of pressure on developing countries or restrict their degree of freedom in policy formulation and implementation.

In future trade negotiations, developing countries should emphasize improvements in the S & D principle, which should be made contractual in all of its dimensions. As a *quid pro quo,* developing countries should be ready to accept internationally agreed and binding criteria for graduation from the special and differential treatment category. Thus, belonging to the category of "developing" would no longer be a matter of self-election. Likewise, developed countries would no longer be able to graduate countries at their own discretion. Countries classified as developing would enjoy access to a truly generalised and universal GSP and temporary derogation from some of the disciplines imposed on developed countries. These derogations would apply to all areas of the agreement. The criteria used for graduation ought to include, besides per capita GDP, indicators of the level of industrial development. In the short term, the S & D principle can be usefully applied, in the process of "tariffication" of NTBs called for in the agreement on agriculture by giving developing countries access to developed country markets at lower bound tariff rates than those applicable to developed country exporters.

The agreement on safeguards has problematic aspects. Close monitoring will be required so as to prevent the major trading partners—and, perhaps, by imitation, some developing countries themselves—from using the loopholes in the agreement (particularly the right to use QRs and the "quota modulation" provision) to reintroduce grey area measures, now under the legal cover of the safeguards agreement. The addition of a clause calling for payment of financial compensation to parties affected by quantitative safeguards when they exceed a certain maximum duration would deter countries from abusing the system. To be sure, the Uruguay Round cannot be considered to have settled the debate on this issue.

The Uruguay Round has given legal sanction to the new protectionism in the form of very unsatisfactory anti-dumping rules. This is an area that will undoubtedly continue to figure prominently on the agenda of future international trade negotiations. As a minimum, all the facts presented to national panels in anti-dumping cases should be subject to review by the Dispute Settlement Board. The use of reconstructed values in determining the existence of dumping and calculating dumping margins should be eliminated altogether. The anti-dumping mechanism would be improved if a clear distinction were made between price discrimination (which ought to be legal) and predatory pricing. The optimal solution would be to eliminate anti-dumping completely and to include the issue of predatory pricing within the framework of competition policy.

Harmonisation of competition policy has often been mentioned as a major item for the post-Uruguay Round trade agenda. Two issues of particular interest to developing countries in this area relate to investment measures and intellectual property. Particular TRIMs—such as export performance, local content, and trade-balancing requirements were seen in the Uruguay Round mainly as trade distortions, although they are also means of offsetting the restrictive business practices of transnational corporations. These practices should be subsumed under efforts to harmonize international competition policies. Similarly, many intellectual property issues impinge directly on competition policy. Impediments to "parallel" imports of patented goods can give rise to questions of competition. A major competition policy issue is the question of the scope and length of patent protection.

Much remains to be done in the area of trade in services. Developing countries ought to press for greater liberalisation of the temporary movement of skilled labour and labour working in the employment of services companies. The initial offers on services in the framework of the General Agreement on Trade in Services (GATS) largely exclude this code of delivery of services to foreign markets, a mode of critical interest to developing countries. Great caution and selectivity needs to be exercised with regard to the liberalisation of financial services; in this respect, the GATS gives developing countries the legal instrument to follow a gradual and selective approach. However, they will have to be prepared to resist bilateral pressures from some of their developed country partners to liberalize their financial services sector too rapidly.

Incorporation into the WTO implies a major domestic challenge for most developing countries. They will have to make efforts to change and adapt domestic legislation in a large number of new areas, including services, intellectual property, and several areas of trade policy that have received little attention in the past (e.g. safeguards, subsidies, and anti-dumping). The enforcement and administrative capacities of national institutions will have to be built up.

The WTO has been given a mandate to include in future negotiations any trade-related subject. The issues of environment and labour standards seem to be first in line. It will not be an easy matter to harmonize policies in these areas.

The reason is that harmonisation can be expected to take the form of aligning policies on developed country standards. It would be naive to pretend that the demands of environmental groups and labour unions on these matters can simply be ignored. Therefore, the challenge ahead is to participate constructively in drafting multilateral rules which expand or preserve access to markets and preclude punitive unilateral action, while taking into consideration environmental and labour concerns.

Overview of WTO's First Year

An important task facing the WTO is that of making the new multilateral trading system truly global in scope and application. While the present membership accounts for more than 90 per cent of world trade, a number of nations are still outside. Many of them have requested accession to the WTO. Twenty eight governments—ranging from China, the Russian Federation, Ukraine, and Vietnam to the Baltic States, Bulgaria, Mongolia, Panama and Vanuatu are at various stages of a process that has become more involved because of the WTO's increased coverage relative to the GATT. With many of the candidates currently undergoing a process of transition from centrally planned to market economies, accession to the WTO offers these countries—in addition to the usual trade benefits—a way of underpinning their domestic reform processes.

Trade Policy Reviews

The 1995 programme extended the coverage to services, intellectual property and other policies covered by the Uruguay Round agreements. Reviews of developed countries have highlighted the generally open nature of their trade policy regimes for industrial products, coupled with a tendency to protect "sensitive" sectors, such as agriculture, textiles and clothing, and to use contingency protection, both of which impose high costs on the rest of the economy. Reviews of developing and transition economies have underlined the progress of autonomous trade liberalisation and the rapid pace of change to enhance economic efficiency through deregulation, privatisation, and more open investment regimes.

Dispute Settlement

Since January 1, 1995, a new dispute follows the procedures of the Dispute Settlement Understanding annexed to the WTO agreement. As is well known, these procedures mark a substantial change from the past. They are a unified set of rules which apply generally to all WTO disputes, the adoption of panel reports cannot be blocked by parties to the dispute, and they provide for the appeal of a panel decision to a new seven-person Appellate Body. The new procedure are overseen by the General Council, sitting as the Dispute Settlement Body.

As of 27 November, the Dispute Settlement Body had been notified of 21 requests for consultation, the step which marks the beginning of a WTO dispute. As these requests by different Members sometimes concerned the same measure, the number of distinct measures subject to disputes was 14. Of these 14, four have been withdrawn, and panels have been established in four.

All cases brought so far have involved goods and GATT 1994. Most of the 21 requests have additionally invoked other goods agreements: Technical Barriers to Trade (seven), Application of sanitary and Phytosanitary Measures (five), Customs Valuation (three), Agriculture (two), and Licensing (two). In one case the General Agreement on Trade in Services has been invoked.

It is too early to draw definite conclusions on the functioning of the WTO dispute settlement system. The total requests for consultations and panels established are roughly on the same level as during 1994 under the GATT. However, the number of disputes (involving different measures) is somewhat less than before in terms of requests for consultation (14 versus 18) and panels established (four versus nine). The parties involved in the disputes are largely unchanged: as before, the United States, the European Communities, Japan and Canada have been the most active participants. Developing countries, however, have been more active as complaints than in the past: Brazil, Chile, Guatemala, Honduras, India, Mexico, Peru, Singapore, Thailand, and Venezuela have been or are all parties to WTO disputes.

Dispute Settlement Under the GATT 1947 and the Tokyo Agreements

During the review period, dispute actions have been initiated or pursued under certain WTO predecessor agreements still in force. Under the GATT 1947, four panel reports EC-Member States' Import Regimes for bananas, EC-Import Regime for Bananas, United States-Restrictions on Imports of Tuna and United States-Taxes on Automobiles) were submitted to the Council for adoption, and there was one new request for consultations (Chile-Taxes on distilled spirits).

Under the Anti-dumping Agreement, one new panel report was adopted (EC-Anti-dumping duties on imports of cotton yarn from Brazil), and one new panel report was circulated (EC-Andi-dumping duties on audio tapes in cassettes originating in Japan). Under the Subsidies Agreement, one panel case was suspended (United States-Countervailing duties on certain carbon steel flat products from several Member states of the EC), one new panel report circulated (United States-Imposition of countervailing duties on certain hot-rolled lead and bismuth carbon steel products originating in France, Germany and the United Kingdom), and one panel report adopted (United States-Countervailing duties on non-rubber footwear from Brazil).

Balance-of-payment Restrictions

By the end of 1995, eleven Members will have held consultations, under Articles XII or XVIII: B of the GATT, with the WTO and/or GATT 1947 Committees. In June 1995, the Committees requested Slovakia to eliminate the 1994 import surcharge by the end of 1995, if possible, but in any case before June 30, 1996. Poland was requested to eliminate in import surcharge established in 1992 by the time of the next consultation, due in June 1996. The Committee recommended to Sri Lanka not to have recourse to the provisions or Article XVIII: B. Consultations were also held with Bangladesh and the Philippines, and consultations with India will be held. Egypt, Israel and South Africa disinvoked the BOP provisions, in July, September and November 1995 respectively.

Hungary made a notification prior to the imposition of an import surcharge on March 20, 1995 and consulted with the Committees in June. The Committees requested Hungary to present a concrete timetable for the reduction and elimination of the surcharge. In July, Brazil invoked Article XVIII: B in respect of a quota on imports of motor vehicles for the second half of 1995. Following the Committees request at consultations held in October 1995, the import quota was withdrawn.

Trade and Environment

During the first part of 1995, the new WTO Committee on Trade and Environment (CTE) reviewed the nine items on its work programme. With respect to three items, the CTE was able to take advantage of and build on the work done by the GATT Group on Environmental Measures and International Trade during 1991-1993: these were the relationship between WTO provisions and trade measures taken pursuant to multilateral environmental agreements (MEAs), eco-labeling and packaging requirements, and the transparency of trade-related environmental measures and environment-related trade measures. Regarding exports of domestically prohibited goods, work in the CTE has also been able to benefit from earlier discussions in GATT. With respect to the other five items in its work programme, discussions in the CTE have often involved examining trade issues from new perspectives.

Where the CTE is charged with addressing the relationship between WTO provisions and trade-related environmental measures or trade measures applied for environmental purposes, discussions have considered a number of policies, related those policies to relevant WTO provisions, and examined how those provisions apply—including whether they provide adequate rules and disciplines to ensure that unnecessary trade restrictions and distortions are avoided. Some delegations have also emphasized the need for the Committee to consider to what extent WTO provisions adequately accommodate trade and trade-related measures serving environmental purposes, and in this respect one proposal has been made to amend and/or interpret GATT Article XX to clarify its relationship to trade measures taken pursuant to multilateral environmental agreements.

The goal of sustainable development is stated several times in the Marrakesh Ministerial Decision of Trade and Environment. Discussions in the CTE on the effect of environmental measures on market access, especially in relation to developing countries (particularly the least-developed) and the environmental benefits of removing trade restrictions and other distortions have indicated a widespread belief that the complementarities between good environmental policy-making and good trade policy-making have a particular potential to promote and accelerate sustainable development. Further liberalisation of trade in goods and in services would allow the same level of output to be produced at less resource cost, generate income that can be used to help pay for environmental protection and conservation, and remove restrictive trade policies that impact adversely on the environment. More broadly, it is evident from the CTE discussions that all believe there is no inherent contradiction between upholding and safeguarding an open, non-discriminatory and equitable multilateral trading system on the one hand, and protecting the environment and promoting sustainable development on the other.

Technical Cooperation and Training

The expanded scope of the WTO has increased substantially the demand for technical assistance. Over sixty national or regional seminars, workshops and technical missions were arranged during 1995. In addition, a total of ninety-nine officials from developing countries and from economies in transition participated in the Trade Policy Courses, covering aspects of trade policy, international trade law and the multilateral trading system. A Workshop on Notification Requirements of the GATT/WTO legal system was held in Geneva, as well as the sixth Special Training Course on Dispute Settlement Procedures and Practices.

Cooperation with Other Organisations

There are two aspects to cooperation between the WTO and other international organisations—the nature of the formal institutional relationships, and the informal cooperative efforts in such as technical assistance and economic research.

As regards the first aspect, an arrangement has been concluded with the United Nations, on the basis of Article V of the WTO and in line with the mandate given by Members, that is consistent with the respective status and mandate of the two organisations (in particular, the contractual nature of the WTO). Under the arrangement, cooperation between the Secretaries will be improved, including new and expanded cooperation between the WTO and United Nations Conference on Trade and Development (UNCTAD).

Another important area of cooperation currently underway or in preparation is the Secretariat's programme of activities for Africa, a result-oriented initiative to help

African countries expand and diversify their trade, to be pursued in a strongly cooperative fashion with other inter-governmental organisations, in particular with UNCTAD and ITC.

Future cooperation between the WTO and UNCTAD will not be limited to the WTO programme of activities for Africa. To enhance cooperation between the two organisations and develop further the already strong complementarity. To work for a greater complementary in technical cooperation—not only between the WTO, UNCTAD and the ITC, but also with other agencies, whether in the UN system, the Bretton Woods organisations, or regional bodies—in order to improve coordination across the board and make better use of resources. It all shows that the WTO's first years performance is upto the expectations.

Revisiting Bretton Woods

Reforming the World Trade and Finance System

That leading trio of major multilateral economic institutions (The International Monetary Fund and World Bank in Washington D.C. and the WTO in Geneva) were created from the ashes of World War II to build a strong, coordinated, international set of economic arrangements. They did well. Their contributions significantly forges systems of cooperation between governments which, in turn, encouraged global economic growth and development.

But, is it time now to revisit Bretton Woods, that location in the hills of New Hampshire, where half a century ago U.S. Treasury Secretary Harry Dexter White, British Economist Lord Keynes and many others set the plans for the post-war multilateral economic system?

The question is not academic. It was being asked recently in an unprecedented scale in the annual meeting of the IMF and World Bank in Washington D.C. The questioning came for three critical reasons:

First, there is a widespread view that a strong supranational institution is urgently required in the currency arena. The IMF has been absorbed with medium-term economics assistance programmes and appears to be attaching low priority to its original purpose. The IMF's Articles of Agreement declare the Fund's purpose is: "To promote international monetary cooperation through a permanent institution which provides the machinery for consultation and collaboration on international monetary problems".

Second, the WTO has brought tempers to the boil in many developing countries and created fears. The WTOs failure is serving now as a stimulus for the growth of regional trade blocs, based upon major industrial countries and open to relatively few developing countries.

Third, the World Bank has taken a backseat when it has come to advancing Western support for the poorest nations. There was a time when the President of the World Bank would use his office to rally international opinion and publicly urge the industrial nations to take a more constructive and more generous approach to the developing nations. In recent times the leadership of the institution has been silent. It has become mired in administrative matters, willing to bow to IMF leadership and content to seek to influence development thinking through the publication of economic research reports.

World Bank Subordinate to IMF

At the same time, the World Bank has come to play second fiddle to the IMF. The Fund has engineered itself into a position of leadership in economic policy discussion with developing countries and with the former command economies of East Europe and Central Asia. The World Bank does not provide programme lending of any kind until a borrowing country first has an IMF programme in place. While the two institutions are totally distinct in legal and financial terms, the Bank has accepted a subordinate position to the IMF.

These three phenomena are not encouraging for the health of global economy and from the perspective, in particular, of the developing countries.

On the monetary front there is a need to protect the interests of developing and emerging countries from the vagaries of the super-economic powers. Most of the governments of the world have looked on hopelessly as Japan, Germany and the United States, have pursued nationalist economic policies that have played havoc with the currency system. Most of the world's trade is booked in the currencies of these three countries and when those currencies spin out of control, so concluding trade deals and securing investment agreements becomes far more complex.

Uncertainty and instability in the world's currency systems are menaces that the IMF was expressly designed to counter. But the IMF has become so engaged in development lending (it now talks of providing programmes to some 80 countries) that its need for financial resources of its own is growing rapidly. That need makes it difficult for the Fund to be critical of its most powerful members. It cannot bite the hands that feed it. Thus, calls to the major nations for fiscal restraint, monetary discipline and international cooperation are made in muted tones.

The Fund, however, must respond to the mounting recognition that some supranational mechanisms are needed to survey the international economic landscape, to ring the alarm bells, to push and shove for meaningful consultation and to place blame on those whose policies are so nationalistic that they endanger the international system. IMF surveillance of the major economic power needs teeth.

The Fund should concentrate once again on using its influence and its expert staff to enhance international understanding of the complexities of the global trading and financial system. By this means it can rebuild its influence with the major powers. While it is unrealistic at this juncture to call for the IMF to become the world's central bank, it could serve as a vitally important convenor of consultative processes designed to attain the objectives that its founders decreed: "To facilitate the expansion and balanced growth of international trade, and to contribute thereby to the promotion and maintenance of high levels of employment and real income and to the development of the productive resources of all members as primary objectives of economic policy".

The IMF's role should be enhanced. It should blend its monetary miles with new trade roles. The WTO been the forum for negotiations and for the supervisions of agreements. WTO does not undertake projects, it does not have powers to influence the policies of its most powerful members and it does not have the prestige needed to provide real leadership. It is time that the WTO was merged into the IMF.

Trade and Finance Belong Together

It makes little sense to split issues of international capital flows from trade questions. The globalisation of trade and investment has brought these disciplines close together. If forging satisfactory agreements is often difficult, then this in part is due to the fact that distinct organisations have leadership for distinct parts (WTO for trade and IMF for money) and there is no effective mechanism for cooperation. It is also the case that within national governments the trade and finance ministries are often in conflict and face insufficient pressure to coordinate. If the IMF managed both trade and monetary negotiations on the global scale, then this would add pressures on trade and finance ministers to work together.

Returning to its original monetary roles and adding a major trade role should be more than enough to keep the IMF busy. It would be logical, particularly in such circumstances, that the Fund return to the World Bank the development financing roles that it has assumed in recent years and that diverted it from its original purposes.

The IMF's Articles stress that one of its purposes is "to give confidence to members by making the general resources of the Fund temporarily available to them under adequate safeguards, thus providing them with opportunity to correct maladjustments in their balance of payments without resorting to measures destructive of national or international prosperity".

The Fund might argue that the World Bank should confine itself to infrastructure and social project finance and technical assistance and leave all programme lending to the IMF. The reality is that the World Bank discovered to an increasing degrees, starting with experiences with Turkey in 1979 and then with many highly indebted nations from 1982 onwards, that the best development projects will fail in countries where wholly unsatisfactory economic policies are in place. The Bank has also recognised the pain and complexity of adjustment and that countries embarking on adjustment policies enter upon a multi-year process: a process better geared to types of financing arrangements that the World Bank can offer, than those provided by the IMF.

Avoid Duplication of Effort between IMF and World Bank

The experiences of the last decade have strengthened the World Bank's understanding of macro-economic policy reform and enhanced its capacity to provide comprehensive policy from support to its member countries. Cooperation with the IMF has improved, but it is also second best option and an expensive one. There remains too much duplication between the Fund and the Bank. The biggest cost is paid by the borrowing countries—ministers and their immediate subordinates spend endless hours negotiating separately with IMF and World Bank teams and developing duplicative reports.

Reform is only necessary when things are not working well. Today there is enormous scope for improvement in the global trading, monetary and development areas. The three prime institutions created for these areas are not performing well enough. Reform is urgent: the WTO should be merged with the IMF, the IMF should refocus on issues fundamental to securing a healthy global monetary (and trading) system and withdraw from the aid game: and the World Bank should have enlarged scope and provide more leadership on the development front.

Such reforms will not end the problems that our world economic system faces and their significance will be largely determined by the support they receive from the leaders of the most powerful industrial nations, irrespective of the zeal of the officials within the IMF and World Bank. Today, in the midst of prolonged international slump where nobody is satisfied with the ways in which the international system is operating, there is an important opportunity to secure backing in the capitals of the world's super-economic powers for the types of reform that are articulated here.

13

Developing Countries After the Uruguay Round

The conclusion of the Uruguay Round (UR) was an important event for the developing countries, for a number of reasons. First, and for the first time a large number of developing countries participated actively in the negotiations comprising the Round. Secondly, the results of the Round are remarkably broad, covering issues such as agriculture, services, and intellectual property rights, which had not previously been brought under GATT auspices. Thirdly, the Final Act of the Round imposes a range of obligations on developing country Governments that is wider and deeper than any previous GATT Round. Moreover, while "special and differential treatment" survives in principle, the Uruguay Round agreements provides few real exemptions for developing countries that are not in the "least developed" category. However, the agreements generally do provide for more generous phase-in-periods; they require the phasing out of the multifibre arrangements (MFA), bring somc clarity to antidumping and safeguard rules, and strengthen the multilateral dispute settlement procedures.

From an old-fashioned perspective where multilateral trade negotiations are viewed purely as a setting for the exchange of concessions, it can be argued that developing countries have not achieved much They are now burdened with a wider range of obligations while their few concrete gains, such as the phasing out of the MFA, are suspiciously back-loaded. However, this is the wrong way to read the significance of the UR for developing countries.

First of all, in a number of important ways the UR agreements promise to strengthen multilateral discipline in world trade. This is especially true in the area of dispute settlement. Under the rules of the World Trade Organisation (WTO), a country will no longer be able to veto a panel's decision which goes against itself. Previously, the adoption of a panel's report on a dispute required an unanimous vote, which meant that any country could block a decision that went against it. Under the WTO, a party to the dispute will be allowed to appeal the panel's decision, but the concerned party will be unable to block the decision of the appellate panel itself. Developing countries have traditionally made very little use of the GATT dispute settlement procedure, preferring to "settle out of court" by taking up offers from the developed-country importers to negotiate quantitative restrictions or price undertakings. The revised procedures should alter this situation, particularly as the new dispute settlement procedure will apply to all areas covered by the WTO, and not just trade in goods.

Secondly, as Governments are increasingly coming to realize, taking advantage of international trade is a good development strategy. From this perspective, most of the developing country "concessions" needs to be entered on the positive side of the balance sheet, and not viewed as a liability. Many Governments in Latin America, for example, have already chosen to undertake unilateral liberalisation measures that go far beyond those which the WTO would require of them. Mexico, Argentina, Bolivia and Chile, to cite some of the more prominent cases, have accepted few obligations that they were not willing to submit of their own accord. For Governments in such countries, the Uruguay Round is nothing but good news. Governments in countries with more hesitant reform may be taking on responsibilities not entirely in line with their current economic philosophies. But perhaps even the latter have come to realize that special preferences for developing countries (as in the case of the Generalised System of Preferences) have largely not worked in the past, and are even less likely to be put to a good test in the future. The more realistic option for all but perhaps the least developed countries is to seek to participate in the WTO as full-fledged members. A good case can be made that equal participation may prove of greater value to many developing countries than special and differential treatment had proved to be in the past.

Finally, there may be some subtle ways in which the UR agreements can help developing country governments to build better structures of governance at home so as to enhance the performance of their economies in areas that go beyond trade. The traditional pattern of state-society interactions in much of the developing world has failed miserably and is in need of rethinking and reform. This goes beyond tinkering with specific polices—such as trade protection or subsidies—and involves altering the manner in which these and other policies are exercised. Too often policy regimes are characterised by uncertainty and lack of credibility, excessive discretion, particularism and favouritism, lack of transparency, and inadequate provision for property rights. These have the effect of stunting production and investment incentives in the private sector. They are much more damaging than price distortions per se.

How can the WTO help? Wisely used, the restrictions placed on economic policy by the UR agreements can assist in overcoming the traditional shortcomings of governance in the developing world. For one thing, the agreements require greater transparency and predictability in many areas of trade policy. Similarly, the wider range of tariff bindings enhances the credibility and predictability of the rules of the game. The new restrictions on the use of QRs in response to payment difficulties limit an important source of discretionary behaviour. The obligations in the areas of TRIMs make it harder for a government to play favourites by differentiating among firms. All of these are meant to ensure that foreign firms are not discriminated against, but their potentially greater payoff may lie in levelling the playing field for domestic firms to compete.

The real threats to developing countries lie in the post-Uruguay Round agenda. Even before the Uruguay Round agreements were signed in Marrakesh, two new issues had reached the top of the trade agenda of developed countries: labour standards and the environment. The developed countries, led by the United States, are intent on seeking some "upward harmonisation" in these areas, which were left out of the Uruguay Round. Whatever the validity of such concerns, the trouble is that they threaten to hit developing countries precisely in products where their comparative advantage is greatest. Ultimately, at stake is nothing less than the comparative advantage of poor countries in labour-intensive and resource-using industries. The dangers are magnified by the obvious reality that both labour and environment standards lend themselves to capture by protectionist groups in developed countries. Alleged concern with labour rights and the environment promises to give such groups the moral high ground, even when their true objective may be none other than old-style protectionism.

In resisting pressures for upward harmonisation in labour and environmental standard, developing countries have many good arguments on their side. First, most careful empirical studies have found that the quantitative importance of social and environmental dumping, if it exists at all, is quite small. Secondly, as the advocates of free trade never cease to point out, nothing works in enhancing labour standards and environmental protection as well as an increase in income levels, which is of course what free trade is designed to achieve. Thirdly, trade restrictions are a very blunt and often counter productive instrument for achieving their stated moral objectives. Fourthly, the experience within the United States and the European Union demonstrates that a high degree of economic integration can coexist with widely varying labour practices and institutions at the level of States or member countries. Fifthly, many environmental concern can be adequately covered with appropriate labelling of imported goods. Finally, since labour and environmental questions go beyond trade relations, these issues should be discussed in their own appropriate multilateral forums and not in the WTO.

These and many other arguments can be deployed to bolster the developing-country case that labour and environmental concerns do not justify trade restrictions or their inclusion in the WTO. However, it may be a mistake for developing countries to believe that the danger will recede if such arguments are repeated often enough. The issues are unlikely to disappear on their own, and developing countries will have to work towards establishing a mechanism whereby legitimate demands can be handled without being hijacked by protectionist interests.

A well-designed social safeguards clause in importing countries is not necessarily inimical to the interests of developing countries. However, such a clause will have to contain two significant provisions. (a) a mechanism to test the legitimacy of the social claim by enlisting exporting and consumer interests in the importing country in the decision-making process; and (b) compensation of the affected exporters, at least in cases where the exporting country possesses a reasonably democratic regime. Such a system will not cost developing countries much. It will have the advantage of engaging the developed countries in a constructive dialogue, and of forestalling the emergence of a new set of "grey area" measures outside of the WTO.

The Uruguay Round

Unravelling the Implications for Low-income and Least-developed Countries

The ministerial declaration which launched the Uruguay Round in September 1986 included as its first objective the expansion of world trade, especially to benefit less developed countries. The principle of special and differential treatment, as set out in various articles and agreements of the General Agreement on Tariffs and Trade (GATT), was to be respected both in terms of the offers made by developed countries and the obligations which developing countries would assume in return. Special attention was to be given to the least-developed countries and ways to promote their trade.

Most evaluations of the Uruguay Round's Final Act, however, suggest that the least-developed countries, and especially countries in sub-sharan Africa will be net losers. This primarily arises from a deterioration in terms of trade as a result of projected increases in food import prices. Beyond a general boost to world demand, the agreements do little to address the problems of other primary commodity exporters, i.e., over-supply, price instability and supply-side difficulties in diversification. In addition, many of these countries will experience erosion of preferential tariff margins in their major export markets and, where preferences do not apply, to persistent (and in some cases increasing) tariff escalation.

On agriculture, most developing counties have a longer time-frame than the developed countries to make fewer subsidy cuts and lower market openings, while the least-developed countries have been exempted from all such commitments. The gains of increased access to export markets as well as gradually rising and more stable world prices for net-exporters of temperate agricultural products will be relatively concentrated unless countries are able to diversify their production. In contrast, higher costs of food imports will become more widespread because a large number of least-developed and low-income countries are net-food importers.

New rules on safeguards and other non-tariff measures will mainly be of interest to larger exporting developing countries, though they have been used against least-developed countries. 'Voluntary' export restraints have been banned and the use of countervailing duties should decline with clarification of 'allowable subsidies', new de minimis provisions, and the exemption of poorer countries from the ban on export subsidies.

Conversely, safeguards may now be applied selectively and without compensation initially, while the use of anti-dumping duties (ADD) seems likely to grow in both developed and developing countries until they are replaced by international competition policy. For all these forms of selective action against developing country produce, however, the duration will likely be shortened with the new requirements for reviews (in dumping and countervail cases) or termination (in the case of safeguards).

For least-developed countries, the new rules on services, intellectual property, and investment imply changes in access to their own markets, a new institutional framework and increases costs, with few offsetting advantages. Whereas more advanced developing countries, especially those with a stronger technological base, will experience new opportunities to export services, there will be limited openings for most least-developed countries' exports of labour services. The rules on intellectual property could slow down the diffusion of technology, while the rules on trade-related investment measures will narrow the choice of industrial policies. In both cases, the least-developed countries have longer to meet the new rules 11 and seven years respectively—rather than any special exemptions.

There are numerous institutional changes arising from the Uruguay Round, both in terms of the way in which the WTO will be managed and its relationships with other organisations, as well as some of its functions, namely dispute settlement and the trade-policy reviews mechanism. On balance, many of these changes will help to bolster the adherence of both large and small countries to international trade rules. But the possibilities of cross-retaliation and cross-conditionality suggest that developing countries will face greater pressures to comply.

Many are already concerned about pressures to extend the WTO to a second set of 'new' issues—the environment, labour and competition policy. The first two issues raise questions about how far differences in national standards reflect national characteristics, and whether trade remedies should be used to offset differences affecting trade or to enforce relevant international standards. Developing countries worry that action against their exports on environmental or labour grounds could seriously devalue the developed countries' market access commitments, in return for which they themselves have accepted significant new obligations. On competition policy, the challenge is to consider whether international rules attached to the WTO can be used to substitute for anti-dumping duties, and also to complement national efforts to curb anti-competitive practices of the private sector.

Finally, there is the issue of compensatory and complementary action. The Uruguay Round agreements, in several places, recognize the need to help developing countries, and especially the least-developed countries, to adapt to the new international trade rules. Various types of help are mentioned, raging from various forms of technical and financial assistance, to improvements in preferential tariffs and possible exemption from import relief measures. These are taken the furthest in two separate ministerial decisions on measures in favour of least-developed countries, and another on least-developed and net-food importing countries.

In every case, however, the legal standing of the developed countries' offers of assistance is unclear—in sharp contrast with the binding obligations assumed by developing countries—while there is no guarantee that it will be additional to existing aid efforts. Existing financing mechanisms for dealing with the adjustment to the Uruguay Round agreements are likely to prove inadequate; the design of alternatives awaits more detailed evaluations of the needs of individual countries. Some developed countries are considering modifications in their Generalised System of Preferences (GSP) and other preferential schemes, but these will be insufficient to offset the erosion of least-developed countries' preferential margins. Moreover new conditions attached to preferences could increase uncertainty and reduce their usefulness. Instead developed countries should consider making GSP binding for the least-developed and low-income countries.

15

The Marrakesh Declaration

Ministers, representing the 124 Governments and the European Communities participating in the Uruguay Round adopted the following declaration. Ministers' salute the historic achievement represented by the conclusion of the Round, which they believe will strengthen the world economy and lead to more trade, investment, employment and income growth throughout the world. In particular, they welcome:

- The stronger and clearer legal framework they have adopted for the conduct of international trade, including a more effective and reliable dispute settlement mechanism;
- The global reduction by 40 per cent of tariffs and wider market opening agreement on goods, and the increased predictability and security represented by a major expansion in the scope of tariff commitments; and
- The establishment of a multilateral framework of disciplines for trade in services and for the protection of trade-related intellectual property rights, as well as the reinforced multilateral trade provisions in agriculture and in textiles and clothing.

Ministers affirm that the establishment of the World Trade Organisation (WTO) ushers in a new era of global economic cooperation, reflecting the widespread desire to operate in a fairer and more open multilateral trading system for the benefit and welfare of their peoples. Ministers express their determination to resist protectionist pressures of all kinds. They believe that the trade liberalisation and strengthened rules achieved in the Uruguay Round will lead to a progressively more open world-trading environment. Ministers undertake, with immediate effect and until the entry into force of the WTO, not to take any trade measures that would undermine or adversely affect the results of the Uruguay Round negotiations or their implementation.

Ministers confirm their resolution to strive for greater global coherence of policies in the fields of trade, money and finance, including cooperation between the WTO, the IMF and the World Bank for that purpose.

Ministers welcome the fact that participation in the Uruguay Round was considerably wider than in any previous multilateral trade negotiation and, in particular, that developing countries played a notably active role in it. This has marked a historic step towards a more balanced and integrated global trade partnership. Ministers note that during the period these negotiations were underway significant measures of economic reform and autonomous trade liberalisation were implemented in many developing countries and formerly centrally planned economies.

Ministers recall that the results of the negotiations embody provisions conferring differential and more favourable treatment for developing economies, including special attention to the particular situation of least-developed countries. Ministers recognize the importance of the implementation of these provisions for the least-developed countries and declare their intention to continue to assist and facilitate the expansion of their trade and investment opportunities. They agree to keep under regular review by the Ministerial Conference and the appropriate organs of the WTO the impact of the results of the Round on the least-developed countries as well as on the net-food importing developing countries, with a view to fostering positive measures to enable them to achieve their development objectives. Ministers recognize the need for strengthening the capability of the GATT and the WTO to provide increased technical assistance in their areas of competence, and in particular to substantially expand its provision to the least-developed countries.

Ministers declare that their signature of the "Final Act Embodying the Results of the Uruguay Round of Multilateral Trade Negotiations" and their adoption of associated Ministerial Decisions initiates the transition from the GATT to the WTO. They have in particular established a Preparatory Committee to lay the ground for the entry into force of the WTO Agreement and commit themselves to seek to complete all steps necessary to ratify the WTO Agreement so that it can enter into force by 1 January 1995 or as early as possible thereafter. Ministers have further more adopted a Decision on Trade and Environment.

Ministers express their sincere gratitude to His Majesty King Hassan-II of his personal contribution to the success of the Ministerial Meeting, and to his Government and the people of Morocco for their warm hospitality and the excellent organisation they have provided. The fact that this final Ministerial Meeting of the Uruguay Round has been held at Marrakesh is an additional manifestation of Morocco's commitment to an open world trading system and to its fullest integration to the global economy.

With the adoption and signature of the Final Act and the opening for acceptance of the WTO Agreement, Ministers declare the work of the Trade Negotiations Committee to be complete and the Uruguay Round formally concluded.

16

Overview of WTO's First Two Years

An important task facing the WTO is that of making the new multilateral trading system truly global in scope and application. While the present membership accounts for more than 90 per cent of world trade, a number of nations are still outside. Many of them have requested accession to the WTO. Twenty-eight governments—ranging from China, the Russian Federation, Ukraine, and Vietnam to the Baltic States, Bulgaria, Mongolia, Panama and Vanuatu are at various stages of a process that has become more involved because of the WTO's increased coverage relative to the GATT. With many of the candidates currently undergoing a process of transition from centrally planned to market economies, accession to the WTO offers these countries—in addition to the usual trade benefits—a way of underpinning their domestic reform processes.

Trade Policy Reviews

The 1995 programme extended the coverage to services, intellectual property and other policies covered by the Uruguay Round agreements. Reviews of developed countries have highlighted the generally open nature of their trade policy regimes for industrial products, coupled with a tendency to protect "sensitive" sectors, such as agriculture, textiles and clothing, and to use contingency protection, both of which impose high costs on the rest of the economy. Reviews of developing and transition economies have underlined the progress of autonomous trade liberalisation and the rapid pace of change to enhance economic efficiency through deregulation, privatisation, and more open investment regimes.

Dispute Settlement

Since January 1, 1995, a new dispute follow the procedures of the Dispute Settlement Understanding annexed to the WTO agreement. As is well known, these procedures mark a substantial change from the past. They are a unified set of rules which apply generally to all WTO disputes, the adoption of panel reports cannot be blocked by parties to the dispute, and they provide for the appeal of a panel decision to a new seven-person Appellate Body. The new procedure is overseen by the General Council, sitting as the Dispute Settlement Body.

As of 27 November, the Dispute Settlement Body had been notified of 21 requests for consultation, the step which marks the beginning of a WTO dispute. As these requests by different members sometimes concerned the same measure, the number of distinct measures subject to disputes was 14. Of these 14, four have been withdrawn, and panels have been established in four.

All cases brought so far have involved goods and GATT 1994. Most of the 21 requests have additionally invoked other goods agreements: Technical Barriers to Trade (seven), Application of sanitary and Phytosanitary Measures (five), Customs Valuation (three), Agriculture (two), and Licensing (two). In one case the General Agreement on Trade in Services has been invoked.

It is too early to draw definite conclusions on the functioning of the WTO dispute settlement system. The total requests for consultations and panels established are roughly on the same level as during 1994 under the GATT. However the number of disputes (involving different measures) is somewhat less than before in terms of requests for consultation (14 versus 18) and panels established (four versus nine). The parties involved in the disputes are largely unchanged: as before, the United States, the European Communities, Japan and Canada have been the most active participants. Developing countries, however, have been more active as complainants than in the past: Brazil, Chile, Guatemala, Honduras, India, Mexico, Peru, Singapore, Thailand, and Venezuela have been or are all parties to WTO disputes.

Dispute Settlement Under the GATT 1947 and the Tokyo Agreements

During the review period, dispute actions have been initiated or pursued under certain WTO predecessor agreements still in force. Under the GATT 1947, four panel reports EC-Member States' Import Regimes for Bananas, EC-Import Regime for Bananas, United States-Restrictions on Imports of Tuna and United States-Taxes on Automobiles) were submitted to the Council for adoption, and there was one new request for consultations (Chile-Taxes on distilled spirits).

Under the Anti-dumping Agreement, one new panel report was adopted (EC-Anti-dumping duties on imports of cotton yarn from Brazil), and one new panel report was circulated (EC-Anti-dumping duties on audio tapes in cassettes originating in Japan). Under the Subsidies Agreement, one panel case was suspended (United States-Countervailing duties on certain carbon steel flat products from several Member states of the EC), one new panel report circulated (United States-Imposition of Countervailing Duties on certain hot-rolled lead and bismuth carbon steel products originating in France, Germany and the United Kingdom), and one panel report adopted (United States-Countervailing Duties on non-rubber footwear from Brazil).

Balance-of-payment Restrictions

By the end of 1995, eleven Members will have held consultations, under Articles XII or XVIII: B of the GATT, with the WTO and/or GATT 1947 Committees. In June 1995, the Committees requested Slovakia to eliminate the 1994 import surcharge by the end of 1995, if possible, but in any case before June 30, 1996. Poland was requested to eliminate an import surcharge established in 1992 by the time of the next consultation, due in June 1996. The Committee recommended to Sri Lanka not to have recourse to the provisions or Article XVIII: B. Consultations were also held with Bangladesh and the Philippines, and consultations with India will be held. Egypt, Israel and South Africa disinvoked the BOP provisions, in July, September and November 1995 respectively.

Hungary made a notification prior to the imposition of an import surcharge on March 20, 1995 and consulted with the Committees in June. The Committees requested Hungary to present a concrete timetable for the reduction and elimination of the surcharge. In July, Brazil invoked Article XVIII: B in respect of a quota on imports of motor vehicles for the second half of 1995. Following the Committees request at consultations held in October 1995, the import quota was withdrawn.

Trade and Environment

During the first part of 1995, the new WTO Committee on Trade and Environment (CTE) reviewed the nine items on its work programme. With respect to three items, the CTE was able to take advantage of and build on the work done by the GATT Group on Environmental Measures and International Trade during 1991-1993: these were the relationship between WTO provisions and trade measures taken pursuant to multilateral environmental agreements (MEAs), eco-labelling and packaging requirements, and the transparency of trade-related environmental measures and environment-related trade measures. Regarding exports of domestically prohibited goods, work in the CTE has also been able to benefit from earlier discussions in GATT. With respect to the other five items in its work programme, discussions in the CTE have often involved examining trade issues from new perspectives.

Where the CTE is charged with addressing the relationship between WTO provisions and trade-related environmental measures or trade measures applied for environmental purposes, discussions have considered a number of policies, related those policies to relevant WTO provisions, and examined how those provisions apply—including whether they provide adequate rules and disciplines to ensure that unnecessary trade restrictions and distortions are avoided. Some delegations have also emphasized the need for the Committee to consider to what extent WTO provisions adequately accommodate trade and trade-related measures serving environmental purposes, and in this respect one proposal has been made to amend and/or interpret GATT Article XX to clarify its relationship to trade measures taken pursuant to multilateral environmental agreements.

The goal of sustainable development is stated several times in the Marrakesh Ministerial Decision of Trade and Environment. Discussions in the CTE on the effect of environmental measures on market access, especially in relation to developing countries (particularly the least-developed) and the environmental benefits of removing trade restrictions and other distortions have indicated a widespread belief that the complementarities between good environmental policy-making and good trade policy-making have a particular potential to promote and accelerate sustainable development. Further liberalisation of trade in goods and in services would allow the same level of output to be produced at less resource cost, generate income that can be used to help pay for environmental protection and conservation, and remove restrictive trade policies that impact adversely on the environment. More broadly, it is evident from the CTE discussions that all believe there is no inherent contradiction between upholding and safeguarding an open, non-discriminatory and equitable multilateral trading system on the one hand, and protecting the environment and promoting sustainable development on the other.

Technical Cooperation and Training

The expanded scope of the WTO has increased substantially the demand for technical assistance. Over sixty national or regional seminars, workshops and technical missions were arranged during 1995. In addition, a total of ninety-nine officials from developing countries and from economies in transition participated in the Trade Policy Courses, covering aspects of trade policy, international trade law and the multilateral trading system. A Workshop on Notification Requirements of the GATT/WTO legal system was held in Geneva, as well as the sixth Special Training Course on Dispute Settlement Procedures and Practices.

Cooperation with Other Organisations

There are two aspects to cooperation between the WTO and other international organisations—the nature of the formal institutional relationships, and the informal cooperative efforts in such as technical assistance and economic research.

As regards the first aspect, an arrangement has been concluded with the United Nations, on the basis of Article V of the WTO and in line with the mandate given by Members, that is consistent with the respective status and mandate of the two organisations (in particular, the contractual nature of the WTO). Under the arrangement, cooperation between the Secretaries will be improved, including new and expanded cooperation between the WTO and United Nations Conference on Trade and Development (UNCTAD).

Another important area of cooperation currently underway or in preparation is the Secretariat's programme of activities for Africa, a result-oriented initiative to help

African countries expanded and diversify their trade, to be pursued in a strongly cooperative fashion with other intergovernmental organisations, in particular with UNTCAD and ITC.

Future cooperation between the WTO and UNCTAD will not be limited to the WTO programme of activities for Africa. To enhance cooperation between the two organisations and develop further the already strong complementary. To work for a greater complementary in technical cooperation—not only between the WTO, UNCTAD and the ITC, but also with other agencies, whether in the UN system, the Bretton Woods organisations, or regional bodies—in order to improve coordination across the board and make better use of resources. If all shows that the WTO's First years performance is upto the expectations.

World Trade Expanded Strongly in 1995, for the Second Consecutive Year

The volume of world merchandise exports rose by a healthy 8 per cent in 1995—down from 9½ per cent the previous year—while the combined value of cross border trade in goods and services broke the $6,000 billion mark for the first time. Volume growth, in 1996, for merchandise exports is expected to slow modestly but still maintain a robust level around 7 per cent.

Other Highlights

- For the sixth consecutive year, trade growth exceeded output growth by a wide margin.
- Among the recently-identified factors behind this trend is the rapid expansion in non-OECD countries of processing trade (assembly of manufactures under special tariff regimes, involving imported components and materials, often in designated export processing zones).
- For the fourth consecutive year Asia's import growth exceeded its export growth.

- Central and Eastern Europe was the most dynamic region for trade, with export and import values up by at least one-quarter.
- Trade in office and telecom equipment—which now exceeds trade in agricultural products of trade in mining products—was again the most dynamic category of manufactures trade.
- Africa and the Middle East recorded their best trade performances in recent years, as exports or mining products picked-up strongly mainly due to higher prices for fuels and non-ferrous metals.
- In value terms, world trade in commercial services increased 14 per cent last year, compared with a 19 per cent increase for merchandise trade. Exports of "other private services"—such as insurance, banking and telecommunications—out-performed exports of tourism and transportation services.

17

Defining the Singapore Message of WTO

The first two years of the World Trade Organisation have been very encouraging. A few key aspects are as follows:

- One success that stands out above all the rest is the strengthening of the dispute settlement mechanism. This is the heart of the WTO system. Not only has its proved credible and effective in dealing with disputes, it has helped resolve a significant number at the consultation stage. Furthermore. Developing countries have become major users of the system, a sign of their confidence in it which was not so apparent under the old system.
- Secondly, the continuing increase in the WTO's membership, emphasizes the vitality of the institution and the multilateral trading system that it embodies. It has now reached 123 members, and there are 30 candidates for accession including some truly major trading partners. It is imperative that it has succeeded in each of these accession negotiations, but in a way which strengthens the system as a whole.
- Thirdly, giving renewed impetus to the completion of critical negotiations towards the multilateral liberalisation in the financial services and telecommunications is very important. The resolve of the Quad countries is an encouraging sign in this respect. Countries at all levels of development have a vital interest in seeing the best possible outcome in

these negotiations. Financial services and basic telecommunications are the arteries and the nervous system of the global economy, and their importance to development prospects is crucial.

- Among the issues that are of particular concern to developing countries, one important concern is textiles. Developing countries do not want to re-write the Uruguay Round Agreement, but they are concerned to see it implemented fully in spirit as well as in letter—which means doing so in a commercially meaningful way. This is a concern which must be taken very seriously.
- Last, but certainly not the least, the progress is now being made towards elimination of tariff on information technology equipment. They have reached and multilateral agreement in this sector at Singapore have succeeded in unlocking one of the key tools of future growth in industrial and developing countries alike.

These are some of the issues that set the stage for developing the WTO's work programme. This means clarifying the steps to renew negotiations in area like services and agriculture which come up at the end of the century. It also means seeing how to approach the commitments which already exist concerning investment, competition policy and government procurement. The immediate task is to build bridges among Members' positions.

Intensive work is beginning to reveal some common ground in a number of areas. For example, the importance of investment, especially for developing countries. Foreign direct investment inflows to developing countries, through their distribution is uneven, increased from an average of about US $22 billion during the second half of the 1980s to about US $100 billion in 1995. And the importance of foreign direct investment goes beyond its mere volume, since it makes available technological, marketing, organisational and managerial inputs to the host country.

The treatment of investment in the multilateral system is still a difficult issue, but there seems to be a broad level of agreement that further work is need—if not on where it should take place.

The Most Thorny Issue

The most thorny issue is labour standards, where the proposals of some Members for work in the WTO have produced clear differences of view. Even here, though, some common ground has been made out in terms of shared principles:

- The respect for core labour standards has been agreed by all Members in the Universal Declaration on Human Rights;
- All delegations have recognised the primary role of the ILO in international labour issues;
- The competitive advantage of low-wage countries has not been called into questions; and
- No-one has opposed statements by major proponents of the issue that trade sanctions are not envisaged.

Even on the basis of these elements, it is easy to reach consensus on this issue, but it is vital that it has not become a divisive or disruptive point at Singapore. The key to reach agreement on the WTO's work programme is to understand that the whole political logic of trade has changed. Especially in the newer areas of the trade universe, industrialised and developing countries are on the same side of the table. In areas like financial services, telecommunications or investment, it is not a question of concessions from one side to the other but of a shared interest in agreeing commitments and rules to the common benefit.

Benefits of Globalisation

This change reflects the inescapable reality of global economic integration. Globalisation certainly presents countries with challenges of adjustment—though these are outweighed by the tremendous opportunities it offers. In many countries it is not uncommon to see a defensive reaction to these challenges, one which plays up the supposed threat from developing country imports or industrialised country investment. How to counter this? By emphasizing the benefits of globalisation and the interdependence it brings with it. The latest UNCTAD report, for example, shows that the outlook for developing countries is generally brighter than for industrialised countries, and in fact developing countries are now an important source of global growth, on which the prospects of the industrialised world more and more depend. In turn, the developing countries depend on industrialised country markets maintaining and improving their openness.

This is why it is so important that Ministers in Singapore sent a strong political message, one which emphasizes the opportunities in the new global economy, which generally do not receive the same emphasis as the challenges. It is a message which recognises the power of the multilateral system as formidable engine for growth in trade, investment and employment.

It is a message about the vital relationship between the multilateral system and regional trade liberalisation, aimed at reinforcing the M.F.N. principle and ensuring that regional and multilateral system converge around it.

Bold Measures for the Least-Developed

And it is a message of unity among industrial and developing countries, and one of determination to help the least-developed countries come in from the margins through bold and specific measures. This last point is particularly urgent need. An interdependent world means that we are all in the same boat together, and no one can watch with equanimity while the other end of the boat sinks.

The G7 leaders at Lyon wisely made the plight of the least-developed countries a priority, and WTO made a proposal to them. Its main features are:

- Full and rapid implementation of the Marrakesh Declaration on the least-developed countries;
- Improving their market access by working towards the elimination of all tariffs and non-tariff barriers on least developed country exports;
- Helping to improve the investment climate they face, especially by creating a more level playing field through negotiating, at the appropriate time, multilateral rules in the WTO.
- Helping to build human and institutional capacity by improving the effectiveness and coordination of technical cooperation. The WTO has made a start in this direction with UNCTAD and the International Trade Centre, and are working hard to improve cooperation with the World Bank and International Monetary Fund. There are especially interesting prospects for extending the reach and the impact of WTO efforts through the use of new information technology, a field where the Bank already has considerable expertise.

One has to encourage a positive consideration of these points inside the WTO and beyond. We have to see a commitment to action along these lines as a very important message of Singapore. In Singapore some of the key questions for global economic development have been on the table. It is essential to reinforce the effort to find the answers together with the partners in the Bank and the Fund.

Africa to Gain More

Trade and Investments from Uruguay Round

New and broader export opportunities and more foreign investments are major benefits Africa is expecting from the Uruguay Round. The lowering of import barriers in the major markets stimulates expansion and diversification of Africa's exports. At the same time, the signing by African countries of the Final Act in Marrakesh has sent a signal to the international business community that they are serious about economic reform—helping attract new investments to the continent.

They are today at the beginning of the transition from the GATT to the World Trade Organisation. This process involves all countries, both the developing and the developed ones. In particular it certainly involves all countries, because a truly global, strong and balanced trading system can only emerge with full and active engagement and support.

The three important key points are:

The first and foremost result of the Uruguay Round is the substantial strengthening of the multilateral trade rules, including the system for setting trade disputes. All trading nations benefit from the order and predictability that come from trade relations based on rules, rather than the rule of economic weight alone. Small and medium-sized nations need the security and protection of clear, fair and effective rules, much more so than the large countries. The second point, often forgotten, is that it gives a badly needed boost to business confidence and help get the industrial countries—who receive 80 per cent of Africa's merchandise exports—back on to a healthy growth path. The third point is that the Round results must be viewed by each participant as a package; on one can claim to have won all the battles.

Critics have charged that there are two principal sources of economic loss for many individual African countries in the final package. The first concerns the impact of reforms of agricultural support policies in OECD countries on international food prices, and thus on the food import bill of countries that are net importers of temperate food products. And the second concerns the so-called erosion of preferential market access opportunities.

Food Imports: A Fuller Assessment

Regarding the first issue, food import bills, forecasts point to increases in the range of 5 per cent in the world prices of certain food products as a result of reforms agreed to in the Round. If these forecasts turn out to be correct, net-food importing countries will pay higher prices for imported food.

In connection to this general issue, it is also important to stress that there will be no "food price shock" similar to the "oil price shocks" of the 1970s, because the reforms will be phased in gradually over six years. Price increases, to the extent that they occur, will come gradually, giving consumers and farmers in the importing countries time to adjust. At the same time, food prices on world markets can be expected to be more stable as a result of the commitment made by major countries to bind policies affecting agricultural products. This is a major benefit to producers and consumers in developing countries, who have experienced wide and sudden variations in the food prices they face as a result of these policies.

In addition, it must be stressed that the response of African farmers, and particularly the farmers in the food-importing countries, will be an especially important part of the overall effects and implications of the adjustment process. By stimulating over-production and subsidised exports, current agricultural policies in the industrial countries harm farmers throughout the developing world, in the food-importing countries no less than in the food exporters. If and to the extent that world prices do rise, domestic food production will increase in these countries, reducing the demand for imported food.

Diversification of Trade

Turning from agriculture to merchandise trade in general, a second point emphasised by critics is the reduction in margins of preference currently enjoyed by developing country exports to industrial countries. The regular GSP schemes are so circumscribed in most granting countries—subject to quota limitations, exclusion of products and conditions for countries to participate—that the increased certainty provided by reductions in bound MFN duties often more than compensates for the reduced margins of preference. ACP preferences are less circumscribed than most GSP schemes. But even then, compensating factors still exist. First, of having improved export opportunities across all products, because product coverage in the Uruguay Round has been rather universal, and this in itself is an element that can be important to many of the countries. And secondly, of having a greater and more secure access to markets other than Europe: as trade barriers come down around the world, African countries should see the geographic destinations of their exports become more diversified, thereby reducing their vulnerability to business-cycle fluctuations in Europe.

Every one is aware of the predictions reached in attempts to quantify the overall impact on African countries of anticipated reforms in agricultural policies and over-all tariff reductions. The usefulness of these impact assessments is often seriously limited by their failure to account for the elimination of quota restrictions, particularly those imposed on exports of textiles and clothing under the Multifibre Agreement.

A serious limitation of the available estimates is their general failure to allow for the future diversification of Africa's production base and foreign trade: diversification into more processing and into appropriate manufactures. Africa's exports remain heavily dependent on primary commodities. Markets for these have been rather depressed since the early 1980s, with many prices at historic lows in real terms. Furthermore, the outlook for most primary commodities points to no substantial reversal of these trends in the foreseeable future.

One must wonder whether the very preferential tariffs granted to certain commodities and other products which surely have been beneficial to the exports in a narrow sense, have not been a major contributing factor in continent's over-concentration on those commodities, which manifestly have little potential to carry economies onto higher plateaus of dynamism and development.

Whilst many may lose some relative margin of preference on unprocessed tropical or natural resource-based commodities, processed forms of these products, as well as manufactures based on them, have benefited from broad and rather deep liberalisation measures and tariff cuts in export markets. In particular, tariff escalation on those two groups of products will fall by an average of around 60 per cent and 30 per cent respectively as a result of the Round. In addition, potentiality to develop more vigorous and broader export sectors will also be enhanced from the strengthening of the rules, that will help guarantee that foreign markets stay really open.

Inspiring Investors' Confidence

Domestic financial constraints have often been a major element preventing the development of the export sector, especially in the least developed countries. Foreign direct investment is increasingly and rightly seen as being of particular assistance in this respect, both for the resource it represents and also because it brings in the technology and experience to successfully complete in world markets.

A major means to stimulate the inflow or foreign investment is to cement the economic reform processes currently underway across Africa. Economic reform eventually creates an investment climate in each country that inspires confidence in foreign investors.

The need to accept the rules, disciplines and obligations laid down in the new WTO has been described by some observers as a burden for developing countries. But economic reorientation in greater or lesser measure will be both a must and an opportunity for all countries taking part in the results of the Round, including Africa. For Africa, the results of the Uruguay Round gives a powerful boost to economic reform, and will send a signal to the international business community that African countries are serious about reform.

Trade and Labour Standards

Using the Wrong Instruments for the Right Cause

A moral value is a shared concern of humanity; hence its enforcement should be a cooperative task implemented for the benefit of humankind. Would we qualify recent approaches to the issue of trade and labour standards as non-inquisitory but shared and cooperatives ones? The purpose of this brief is to shed some light on this question.

In fact, nobody, will deny any country the right to raise and fight for issues which are of moral concern for humanity, as they are supposed to benefit humankind. The issue of implementing and enforcing a core of labour standards one of these.

However, a problem remains: who has the negotiating power to raise and impose them? The key issue is that trade coercive attempts by some become inquisitorial as soon as they are backed by moral concerns which are supposed to be shared by all, while the same "all" lack the negotiating power to be, in turn, coercive if they so wish. In other words, trade related coercion forcedly becomes "inquisition" when moral concerns are introduced into the functioning of an international trading system characterised by large imbalances in the negotiating power of the participating countries. Only a few Government have the negotiating leverage and strength to develop what we may qualify as "trade-related inquisitory practices".

The issue of trade and labour standards seems to have arisen when "uniform competition" has been regarded as a threat to employment and economic growth in some industrial countries.

However, without attaining a certain degree of international agreement and coherence as to whether and under what conditions—a given competitive advantage is, or is not, related to social or other conditions, and whether or not it may be considered as "unfair". With protectionist views in mind, such an approach may only be interpreted as "unbenign thinking" coming from "unfair competitiveness seekers".

If the motivation behind the introduction and further use of moral argumentation is to seek a justification for the possible use of trade measures as enforcement mechanisms to achieve certain goals. Particularly for harmonisation of labour standards, one may wonder why the labour standards issue has not been linked to North-North trade in the current debate on the considerable variation in labour standards among developed countries. The motivation may well be that in the post-Uruguay Round era, when tariffs have been reduced substantially and "grey area measures" put under stricter control or even banned, we may be facing the possible revival of new forms of protectionism wearing "blue", "green" or "multicolour" masks. On the contrary, if the motivation behind the introduction of such moral labour rights argumentation reflects a real commitment by the international community to enforce labour standards, a door may be open for embarking, in the future, on a series on international initiatives, not necessarily under the trade umbrella.

It should also be stressed that the linkage between trade and labour standards has been seriously misinterpreted. Most analysts remain blind to the two-way character of the link between trade and labour standards. On the one hand, trade liberalisation is to promote growth and development by promoting a more efficient allocation of resources and to ease the adoption and implementation of labour standards, as well as to promote job creation. On the other hand—and this is extremely important—raising labour standards—not keeping them low—should increasingly be seen as the real source of competitiveness and economic growth through, among others, increase in the quality of labour. There is a case for considering economic progress and the rise in labour standards as mutually reinforcing.

Turning to the low labour standard debate, much more empirical and analytical evidence is needed to assess the extent to which low labour standards are correlated to lower wages and labour costs. Although raising labour standards may not primarily be intended to maximize efficiency, it is becoming increasingly evident that efficiency and the future potential of the firm may not necessarily be maximised by keeping labour standards low. In this context, it is the development to human capital in LDCs which is a top priority, not because failing to respect labour standards in these economies threatens the welfare of the workers in the industrialised countries but, more simply, because it is the only strategy for enhancing the productivity of labour and ultimately increasing the people's standard of living. Thus, if raising labour standards and ensuring their effective implementation is important for economic progress, developed and developing countries, as well as wokers and employers in each region, should adopt a cooperative, not confrontational, approach in order to deal with this urgent and pressing problem. For this very reason, adherence to trade sanctions would be a wrong approach. Trade is essential for enhancing worker's productivity because it ensures that a country's resources will be employed in the activities that it is best at. In turn, increased productivity is the key to development, higher labour standards and higher wages. Moreover, the issue of labour standards is of a moral nature: it has an undeniable development dimension which needs to be more clearly perceived but, as discussed, it is certainly not an issue to be dealt with through trade measures.

Labour standards should be dealt with in the WTO. The capacities of the ILO will prove invaluable for renewed multilateral effort to improve working conditions in developing countries. Its tripartite structure has proved to be the best suited to the tasks of conciliation and dialogue.

Improving the standards of living and labour standards for workers or eradicating child labour is what matters it is the right cause for humankind, a cause to fight for, through various approaches and by using all the mechanisms at our disposal in order to ensure its success. Thus, the issue is not one of trade and labour standards, but of labour standards and economic development, an issue of a human dignity and human rights nature. It is a universal issue, the solutions to which should be found by all nations, taking into account equity considerations. Each country should participate in the process, depending on its level of economic development. It is precisely because economic development, including trade, is positively correlated with the adoption and effective implementation of labour standards that solutions to low labour standards should not necessarily come from negative and coercive approaches. Solutions for universal problems must not only be efficiency-based but also equity-based. Therefore, the case is for cooperation rather than coercion and for applying positive instruments. As in the case of environmental issues, developing countries should be recipients of funds, technical cooperation and other similar forms of support when the implementation of labour standards involves an inequitable cost burden.

The initiative of "grouping" a core of existing conventions into a new global convention on core labour standards of universal value may, in view of its new and distant qualitative nature, generate strong support from the international community for its implementation. The ILO was created to promote workers' right, so the initiative could be launched under its aegis, in direct collaboration with other intergovernmental organisations dealing with social, trade and development issues in an interrelated manner. The support to this or other similar approaches by the international community, and in particular by those developed countries that have recently shown a special and strong interest in the reinforcement and implementation of labour rights in developing countries, will be a clear sign of their degree of sincerity and their willingness to share the social concerns of universal value which seem to be of paramount interest to most of their citizens.

Caught in the Debt Trap?

The Foreign Indebtedness of Developing Countries

The question of whether there is a way out of the developing countries' debt trap can only be properly answered if their indebtedness is not viewed as an isolated factor. It should be seen in the context of the total net resource flows into these countries. The following facts must be borne in mind:

1. Net resource flows to developing counties increased from 1994 to 1995 by 11.5 per cent of US $231.3 bn. The greatest share was made up of private sector flows, which accounted for 72 per cent ($ 167.1 bn) of total transfer inputs.

2. Of the private flows, foreign direct investments totalling $90.3 bn dominate. Their well above average increase reflects the globalisation of production and growing integration of developing and transformation countries in the world economy. To date, however, this has applied mainly to 12 countries on which about 80 per cent of private inflows is concentrated. These are China, Mexico, Brazil, South Korea, Malaysia, Argentina, Indonesia, Thailand, Russia, India, Turkey and Hungary.

3. Portfolio equity flows to developing countries known for their high sensitivity on earnings and policy have dropped markedly for the time being to $22 bn. This is not a unexpected reaction to.

- the sharp rise in US interest rates since February 1994 and a very positive trend on the American capital market.
- the Mexican peso crisis which began in December 1994; and
- the more cautious evaluation of the risks of investments in emerging markets, which major institutional investors believe have reached a certain degree of saturation.

4. Official development finance totalled $64.2 bn of which the World Bank reported $11 bn was allocated to the rescue action for Mexico alone. ODA in 1995 stagnated at $47 bn. Its proportion of the OECD donor countries' GDPs was 0.29 per cent, the lowest since the beginning of the 1970s. The main reasons for this downturn were the industrial nations' well-known public budget problems and the fact that more creditworthy development and transformation countries are increasingly procuring their finance on private capital markets. Understandably, large sums were made available, mainly by Germany, to Eastern Europe and the successor states to the former Soviet Union. From strictly developmental viewpoints, it is disquieting that ever fewer ODA funds are available for longer-term development projects due to their disbursement for short-term emergency and crisis assistance.

The Washington Decisions

The recent annual conference of G7 finance ministers and central bank chiefs took the following decisions:

1. About 20 highly indebted poor countries (HIPCs) were to be reviewed to establish whether in endeavouring to solve their debt problems they could expect greater support from the international donor community than previously. There was a justified fear that without enhanced assistance, and continuing to employ only the

instruments used to date, these countries would not even achieve an acceptable level of indebtedness within the next 5-10 years.

2. *Time horizon:* In two three-year stages, a comprehensive review of the indebtedness and adjustment measures the affected countries could cope with would be undertaken. This would include observing the impacts of employing the customary instruments of debt relief. If the results were unsatisfactory, the new measures decided in Washington, which were expected to achieve a positive breakthrough, would be applied as well after three to six years. In detail, these are:
   - *Paris Club (official creditors):* Rescheduling of bilateral debts, with case-to-case remission of up to 80 per cent compared with a current ceiling of 67 per cent;
   - Comparable relief conditions through non-Paris Club and private creditors (London Club);
   - *IMF:* Grants from the Enhanced Structural Adjustment Facility (ESAF) or long-term ESAF loans. The recipient countries use these sums for debt servicing; and
   - Redemption of multilateral debts from a future HIPC trust fund to be administered by the IDA. Setting up the fund will formally ensure that it is not a matter of debt remission.

3. *Financing:* Provisional estimates put the cost of the HIPC initiative at around $6 bn. This is to be funded by the Paris Club members, third-party creditors and international finance institutions. Two factors of the total costs are uncertain.

These are the number of countries which in the end will be given access to the funds, and the realism of the estimates of export income upon which the country analyses are based.

4. *Assessment:* All in all, the HIPC initiative is a fresh attempt to substantially relieve these countries of their debt problems, and support their economic reform programmes and measures to alleviate poverty. The World Bank and IMF were directed to begin implementing the debt initiative without delay and report back to the conference of the supervisory bodies in the spring of this year. Leading donor countries were able to agree to the initiative because:
   - financial integrity, particularly the preferential creditor status of the World Bank, the IMF and the regional development banks, was not in question;
   - the debtor countries were not relieved of their basic responsibility for comprehensive and sustainable adjustment policies; and finally;
   - the usual case-to-case procedure, taking decisions from country to country, was retained.

Global Impacts

To complete the "indebtedness picture", two other important problem areas must be pointed out. The problems and risks arising from the HIPCs' indebtedness affect first and foremost the national and, at worst, the regional level of the countries concerned. A serious endangering of the global finance and currency system must not be allowed to emanate from them. However, and this is the first problem, it can be much graver in the case of advanced developing countries, as Mexico showed in 1995. The risks which arise for the money and capital markets from liberalisation of short-term movements of capital in a number of threshold countries with large issue volumes are considerable. Strictly speaking, the capital market securities acquired in these markets by nationals and foreigners are only partly foreign debts. However, because they can be sold at any time and their convertibility and transferability is guaranteed, they can present similarly high risks for the solvency of the country concerned as "traditional" foreign debts. Additionally, the fact that "maturity" here depends not on contractually agreed terms, but on fragile investor confidence, enhances, the risks.

The large sums deployed in the Mexico rescue action organised by the USA and IMF show that endangerment of the international finance system was on hand. Above all, what the financial world aptly labelled the "Tequila effect"—a chain reaction of investors making a mass flight out of other threshold countries such as Brazil, Argentina and the Philippines, which threatened to spread—called for comprehensive confidence-building measures.

Not least, this experience was the basis for the agreement by the G7 ministers and central bankers in Washington on initial steps of a new IMF crisis financing mechanisms. Thus, the General Agreement on Credits was doubled to Special Drawing Rights of $34 bn.

Conclusions

The conclusions that must be drawn from this development are:

- To strengthen the IMF's role as a catalyst and improve its surveillance function;
- To bring the G7 group in their own interest to put in place stable economic general conditions, above all harmonised control of the interest rates of the key currencies; and
- To support the threshold countries in creating credible political conditions, especially by stabilizing their economic, financial and currency policies in order to give no cause for sudden crises of confidence.

21

WTO has Delivered

The Singapore Ministerial Conference has been an outstanding event in all respects. Practically all the WTO Members and Observers have been represented by Ministers.

Unlike most of its GATT predecessors, this Conference is not about the start or completion of a major round of trade negotiations. Indeed, the Singapore Ministerial Conference represents an important point on a continuum in the growth and evolution of the multilateral trading system. The Ministerial Conference is not only the supreme executive body of the WTO but it is also the forum to provide political guidance and overall coherence for the new trading system which was established just under two year ago. In this sense, the Ministerial Conference, in institutional terms, is the cornerstone of the global trading system. It embodies, institutionally, the vision of Ministers at Marrakesh that the WTO should function as a common institutional framework, bringing all countries together from all corners of the world and from all levels of development.

Expansion of the Trading System

The establishment of the WTO, the first major international institution to be created in the post-Cold War era, has resulted in several important advantages for all. The biggest gain of the post-Marrakesh era is the existence and expansion of a trading system based on internationally agreed and enforceable rules and disciplines to both oversee and guarantee progress in international trade. The establishment of the WTO is deservedly see as the outstanding international achievement of the decade to which all Member countries made substantial contributions. It has been widely noted that the credibility and effectiveness of the new system rests on Member governments' full compliance with the rules, disciplines and commitments resulting from the Marrakesh Agreement.

The central focus of the WTO's work in 1995 and 1996 has been the implementation and follow-up of commitments. It is broadly recognised the continual, day-to-day efforts are required by all Members to consolidate the Uruguay Round results and ensure full compliance which are essential to the proper functioning of the system. In systemic terms, the WTO's reinforced dispute settlement mechanism has proved its effectiveness and can be justly regarded as an outstanding success of the Oranisation's first two years.

Labour Standards

The Ministerial Declaration which all have just adopted as a whole has a number of very significant components which provide the necessary balance of interests. All the issues reflected in the Declaration are equally important.

In the first place, with regard to Core Labour Standards—all have agreed on a text which sets out a balanced framework for how this matter should be dealt with. The text embodies the following important elements: First, it recognizes that the ILO is the competent body to set and deal with labour standards. Second, it rejects the use of labour standards for protectionist purposes. This is a very important safeguard for the multilateral trading system, and in particular for developing countries. Third, it agrees that the comparative advantage of countries, particularly low wage developing countries, must in no way be put into question. Fourth, it does not inscribe the relationship between trade and core labour standards on the WTO agenda. Fifth, there is no authorisation in the text for any new work on this issue. Sixth, the WTO and the ILO Secretariats will continue their existing collaboration. The collaboration respects fully the respective and separate mandates of the two Organisations. Some delegations had expressed the concern that this text may lead the WTO to acquire a competence to undertake further work in the relationship between trade and core labour standards.

Integrated Approach on Development

In a gesture of solidarity with the least developed countries, Ministers have recognised the need to pay special attention to the interests of the least developed countries in each of the new issues. They have further recognised the need to provide predictable and favourable market access conditions for least developed countries products, to foster the expansion and diversification of their exports to the markets of all developed countries; and in the case of relevant developing countries in the context of the Global System of Trade preferences.

During the Conference, a number of WTO Members have agreed to tariff elimination for trade in information technology products on an MFN basis. Ministers have welcomed this initiative which, represents an important step towards trade liberalisation in one of the most dynamic sectors of trade in goods.

Overall, at this first Ministerial Conference, the survey of the achievements of the first two year of the WTO's existence and the discussion of the challenges all face in the future have made clear the importance of the issues that have been on the table. The Conference has provided a strong political message underlining opportunities in the new global economy while not ignoring the challenges that the economies face. The message this Conference has sent is one of confidence in the multilateral trading system as it approaches its fiftieth anniversary in 1998 and in its ability to promote growth and guarantee stability.

Few Signs of Hope in Africa

In 1996 a dozen countries in Africa achieved the targetted 6 per cent annual growth in gross domestic product (GDP), while the number of countries suffering from negative growth rates dropped from 19 in 1992 to three in 1996. These figures sound a lot less positive, however, if one compares GDP growth rates with population growth figures. Africa is still far ahead of other developing regions in the world in that respect and continues to grow at annual rates of 2.9 per cent. This means that the continent's estimated total population of 750 million (1996) will double to 1.5 billion by the year 2025. Whatever economic progress can be achieved until then, will have to be shared among an ever greater number of people. From 1991 to 1996 for instance, only 17 countries managed to expand their economies faster than their populations. In 35 countries, this was not the case. Their populations grew faster than their economic production or, in other words, even with modest economic advances, the population as a whole was worse off at the end of the period. On average, Africa's GDP grew by 2.3 per cent in 1996—not such a bad result when compared, for instance, with that of industrialised Europe. But when considering the 2.9 per cent population increase, the continent was left with an actual per capita income decline of 0.6 per cent.

If Africa wants to get out of this spiral of growing poverty, its government must do everything in their power to bring down the increase in their populations. However, a slow-down in population growth will not be enough to help Africa get out of its economic misery, especially since demographic changes are extremely weak as a partner in international economic relations, and the situation seems to be getting worse. Its share of world trade has fallen from 3.1 per cent in 1990 to 2.1 per cent in 1996. The continent still relies for its export earnings on a handful of primary commodities, among them oil, minerals, timber and agricultural goods. But the long-term trend for these commodities is not very promising, given stiff competition from Asia and Latin America and slackening demand in industrial countries. World trade is no longer in commodities—their share in total exports dropped from 25.9 per cent (1990) to 19 per cent (1996). But Africa has not been able to keep up with its competitors from other developing countries who diversified their exports and trading partners and switched to the export of processed goods and manufactures.

The liberalisation of trade after the conclusion of the Uruguay Round is seen in Africa as a danger rather than a chance: estimates are that Africa will initially lose up to 3 billion dollars a year due to Uruguay, mainly from hikes in import bills, budget deficits, and the loss of preferences with the European Union. Unfortunately, the poor trade performance of Africa on world markets is in no way compensated by trade among African countries. Despite numerous efforts in recent decades to promote intra-regional trade, poor roads, railways, waterways and communications have prevented any significant progress in this regard. One of the biggest obstacles to increased regional trade is lack in diversification, which has resulted on too many countries producing the same or similar commodities.

When the New Africa Development Agenda was launched six years ago, the UN Secretary General has estimated that Official Development Assistance (ODA) to Africa would have to be raised to 30 billion dollars for 1992, with a subsequent annual increase of 4 per cent. This target has proved to be illusionary. In actual fact, ODA barely reached 23.5 billion in 1995 and has continued to decline ever since. Although multilateral institutions increased their lending for Africa, the fall in bilateral funds could hardly be compensated.

Private finance also largely neglected Africa as a target for investments. In spite of the political and economic reforms implemented under structural adjustment programmes in no less than 37 African countries, entrepreneurs apparently found it safer and more profitable to invest their money in East Asia, Eastern Europe or Latin America. Of the 60 billion dollars in foreign direct investment (FDI) that went to developing countries in 1996, only 2.1 billion ended up in Africa. The share of the African continent in FDI dropped from 10 per cent (1987-91) to only 3.6 per cent now.

All these are rather depressing figures which are hardly able to inspire new confidence in the future of the continent. One signal of hope, however, comes from the recent annual meeting of thc International Monetary Fund and the World Bank in Washington. After protracted negotiations among creditor nations, an agreement has now been concluded to alleviate the debt burden of poor countries, many of them in Africa. The initiative which will lead to debt cancellations of some 7 billion dollars aims at bringing the debt service burden down to "sustainable" levels. Compared to the total indebtedness of Africa—which now stands at some 314 billion dollars—the amounts in question may seem insignificant. For some of the most heavily indebted countries, however, the scheme may provide the urgently needed breathing space which will allow the benefitting country to make a new start.

The Midterm Review of progress achieved under Africa's New Development Agenda is anything but encouraging. The UN Secretary General has responded to the challenge by launching yet another effort—a Special Initiative on Africa—to mobilise support for the region. The special initiative is built on 20-priority action programmes focusing on water, basic education, health and capacity building for governance and food security. Whether this programme will be able to attract more international support than its predecessors remains to be seen. More likely than not, the present international apathy concerning Africa's development will persist. It is ironical that the once much maligned Bretton Woods institutions are now the most reliable partners of Africa, while for bilateral donors, the continent is slowly drifting away.

23

Trading Towards Peace

The reason why trade has such a vital part to play in building peace is because it means lowering barriers—not only to goods and services but among nations and peoples. The elimination of barriers creates interdependence and interdependence creates solidarity. The history of the last fifty years has shown us all the undeniable benefits of lowering trade barriers and opening economies.

Clearly every region has its own characteristics, and it would be wrong to imagine that the same blueprint can apply everywhere and in the same way. Any region which was for thousands of years at the crosswords of world trade should regain its place in the centre, because doing so will help build peace as well as prosperity. This is why the numerous applications for accession to the WTO from various countries are so significant. The first is through regionalism. There are several efforts at regional trade and economic initiatives among countries, and that such initiatives will be encouraged to reduce positive results. Regional initiatives are important because they can help countries at a comparable level of development to move relatively quickly in opening their economies and in deepening their interdependence.

However, the rapid advance of global economic integration means that while regional initiatives remain important, they are not sufficient by themselves to address successfully the new perspectives of the international economy. That is why there is a need for second track, which is the rule-based multilateral system. And that is why the multilateral system is of fundamental importance to the economic prosperity of any region.

As the first major international institution to be created in the post-Cold War era, the WTO offers a promise of the kind of global economic architecture which need in the coming decades. Its culture is firmly rooted in the tradition of consensus-building and cooperation among sovereign countries. And the WTO embodies rights and obligations negotiated by consensus, approved and ratified by each government and each parliament, and they are enforceable, not through the crude exercise of economic power, but through the rule of law. The alternative would be a power-based system—who would want to chose this option?

But most importantly, the WTO is an organisation which brings all countries—from all corners of the world and from all levels of development—together as equals. There is no weighted voting, no exclusive clubs, no inner and outer circles. Developing countries representing 80 per cent of constituency sit as equals with industrialised countries to write the rules of a shared trading system.

This new unity of developing and developed countries inside a single system will be credited as the greatest achievement of the multilateral system. But this unity is still fragile: we cannot allow it to be broken. This is why, in preparing the agenda of the first Ministerial meeting in Singapore, have recognised particularly the difficult task facing developing countries in implementing the Uruguay Round Commitments. They have also acknowledged the challenges they face in contemplating the necessary work programme.

The integration of developing countries as equal partners in the multilateral system is one of the most important challenges in shaping the economic order of the 21st century. This is a shared responsibility of developed and developing countries alike. There is no rational alternative to this objective. The evolution of the global economy makes that clear.

Now there is a need to work together as equal partners to ensure the full integration, and all other developing and transition economies, into the global economy and the rule-based multilateral trading system. In conjunction with this there is a need to encourage, notably with growth of regional economic cooperation. The alternative is a vicious circle where economic isolation feeds greater political instability which in turn leads to greater economic isolation. The road to a lasting peace in the world begins, not ends, with economic integration and interdependence. Taking this message to heart will help build a future where it is goods, services, and investment that cross borders—not missiles and soldiers.

Free Trade as Peacemaker

The Benefits of an Open World Trading System

Globalisation by free trade according to the principles of the World Trade Organisation (WTO) offers the only realistic opportunity to integrate the world peacefully and in time to prevent a major disaster. The primacy of the economy over politics is the most important vehicle for a successful world domestic policy.

Since Adam Smith, traditional economic theory has on principle been well-disposed towards free trade. Free trade enables better use of the world's economic resources than does national protectionism. Countries can concentrate on their respective strength and draw from their trade partners the goods they need, but do not produce. But there have always been objections against free trade.

The international trade system has always been encumbered by disperate accusations of unfair competition. The fear that foreign competitors use unfair methods, such as dumping, as and is widespread. If one were to believe all the charges of dumping that are made, then international trade would have been completely destroyed long ago. Great restraint should be exercised with respect to allegations of dumping if one is interested in maintaining an interweaving of international economic activities.

The Free Trade Opposition Cloaks Itself in Dumping Charges

The modern form of the struggle against free trade

cloaks itself in the accusation of ecological dumping or social dumping. With this difficult subject matter, one should not make sweeping generalisations. These things also are not gone into in detail in what follows.

Environmental protection is an asset that every economy produces at the cost of other assets. The people's preferences for the asset of environmental protection probably varies from country to country. It is also completely legitimate and does not at all distort trade if the environmental provisions—in line with the different national preferences—vary from country to country.

In the rich western European economic region, one should guard against a new form of cultural imperialism. It is not for this part of the world to impose its preferences for environmental assets on other countries, especially Third World countries. Free world trade brings not only economic advantages. Even more important is its contribution to lasting world peace.

In view of world population growth, every standstill in the movement towards a peaceful world society must be seen as a step backwards. We are compelled to run a race between the growing problems and the development of stable institutions to overcome them peacefully at global level. Economic history since the end of the World War II shows clearly that free trade under the old GATT was of decisive importance for the prosperity of the industrialised nations.

The principle of help for self-help has nowhere been applied so consistently as on the free world market. In reverse, the examples of countries that cut themselves off from the world market show the disastrous consequences of the rigidity of a society which shuns the pressure of international competition.

Revolutionary Success of Open-Market Policies

The West's policy of open markets pursued since 1948 and reinforced since 1989 has led to a dynamism which, in the true meaning of the word, is revolutionary. More than half the world population now lives in countries with annual GDP growth rates of more than 5 per cent. Europe is not among that group, which may be why it also stands somewhat apart in its mentality.

Certainly, there can also be undesirable trends in free trade. There is no ideal systems; one must choose between imperfect potentialities. However, no realistically better substitute for the free trade system is in sight, not even with respect to the goals of a pacified world: an ecological sound world economy and a balance of global dimensions between the poor and the rich. An ideal government of philosopher kings armed with absolute power certainly could do something better than does free trade—but such a government remains fictitious. There are tangible and narrow limits to what the political system, whether democratic or not, can effect in a positive sense. This is how the structural conservatism of democratic and other political systems impedes the timely assertion of reforms necessary to achieve a world peace society.

The GATT was turned into the World Trade Organisation (WTO) a few years ago. Besides extending the free trade principle to services and additional agricultural sectors, the new agreement foresees above all the full inclusion of the Third World in the system. The agreement commits the industrialised nations to open their markets to developing and threshold countries.

Other important points are the strengthening and tightening of the dispute mediation process. Based on a system of relatively independent ad hoc panels, it permits complaints against WTO member countries for violations of the agreement. Thus, what is arising here is an effective global jurisdiction within the meaning of a peaceful world domestic policy.

Exclusion as Penalty

The decisive sanction mechanism of the WTO—which is not a specialist organisation of the United Nations—is the threat of exclusion. Exclusion would deny the penalised country free access to the markets of WTO members on the basis of most favoured nation status. This is a threat that requires no armed force, but is very effective. No country can still afford to do without the beneficial effects on prosperity that participation in international trade brings.

Thus, with the threat of denial of access to world markets for violating WTO rules, and the guarantee of a more or less fair competition for a country's own products for abiding by them, a non-military sanctions system has come into being. That is substantial progress on the path to a pacified world.

Certainly, this sanction system's sphere of influence is limited for the time being. Essentially, it will be used to assert the game rules of free trade. It offers no legal grounds for pressing other goals, such as on human rights. Attempting to expand it in this direction would for the foreseeable future put the entire system at risk.

In the current debate on globalisation, the question arises of whether the world economic institutions should not be converted in this manner, that politics regains its autonomy, and that the primacy of politics can be restored. The critics of globalisation point to the constraints to adjust which the world economy exercises on national or continental politics. However, well this demand for the primacy of politics may be justified in philosophical terms, it virtually comes down to a demand for the ascendancy of the conservative principle.

Danger of a Slowed-Down World Integration

The demand for the primacy of politics is gaining strength from the desire to avoid the pressure to adjust which the dynamics of world events are exerting. It is today a conservative, and in fact a reactionary, longing for the (Utopian) return of the functioning European welfare state of two or three decades ago. If it were asserted, it would mean practically slowing down world integration. It would run dead against the goal of a world policy based on a desire for peace.

The present primacy of the economy over politics—in terms of the free movement of goods, services and capital—is basically nothing more than the priority of the global principle over the provincial, the national principle. As such, it gives the principle of change pre-eminence over the principle of maintaining the status quo. What gives the primacy of the economy its legitimacy? Probably not the thought that world peace and better be secured by this means. Its legitimation lies in the very indirect economic success that the free trade system delivers. For the reflective observer, the question remains of whether this legitimation is sufficient.

To answer this question, however, and particularly if one pleads for maintaining the ascendancy of the economy, it appears appropriate to outline the consequences that can be expected from further integration of the world economy. As can be seen today in East and Southeast Asia, the growth dynamics of the world economy will lead to a marked rise in the living standards of a large part of the Third World.

Do not Exclude Poor Countries from the Competition

The global consequences of Asia's growth should not have been seen only negatively. While it may also mean, for example, a great burden on the global climate, it leads at the same time to an acceleration of the process of falling birth rates and thus to an earlier stabilisation of the world population. Prosperity for the Third World is so far the only realistic answer to the urgent problem of population growth. And free competition on the world market in the only reliable means of achieving this prosperity in the course of some decades.

Despite ecological sacrifice in the medium term, continuation of Third World growth is the only way to solve the long-term ecological problems. One also should not forget that only those who can eat their fill and have a roof over their heads are prepared to reflect on ecology and discuss it.

As for the rest, the balance between rich and poor is more acceptable when the poor become richer than when the rich become poorer. That applies also at the international level. The market and access to it are peaceful sanctions of the world economic system on the basis of free trade. Those who are hungry and have nothing more to lose are more of a danger to world peace than those who have eaten their fill. The ruse of covering up domestic problems by cross border military aggression will become less attractive to the degree that a country's own economy is integrated in the global economic system. The more countries are economically dependent on each other, the more unlikely it is that they will wage war on each other.

Globalisation by free trade according to the principles of the WTO offers the only realistic opportunity to integrate the world peacefully and in time to prevent a major disaster. The primacy of the economy is the most important vehicle for a successful world domestic policy.

The Uruguay Round and Agricultural Reform

The Uruguay Round of Multilateral Trade Negotiations (completed in 1994) continued the process of reducing trade barriers achieved in seven previous rounds of negotiations. Among the Uruguay Round's most significant accomplishments were the adoption of new rules governing agricultural trade policy, the establishment of disciplines on the use of Sanitary and Phytosanitary (SPS) measures, and agreement on a new process for setting trade disputes. The Uruguay Round also created the World Trade Organisation (WTO) to replace the General Agreement on Tariffs and Trade (GATT) as an institutional framework for overseeing trade negotiations and adjudicating trade disputes. Agricultural trade concerns that have come to the fore since the Uruguay Round, including the use of genetically engineered products in agricultural trade, state trading, and a large number of potential new members, illustrate the wide range of issues any new round may face.

During the past years since initial implementation of the Uruguay Round agreements, the record with respect to agriculture is mixed. The Uruguay Round's overall impact on agricultural trade can be considered positive in moving toward several key goals, including reducing agricultural export subsidies, establishing new rules for agricultural import policy, and agreeing on disciplines for Sanitary and Phytosanitary trade measures. The Uruguay Round

Agreement on Agriculture (URAA) may also have contributed to a shift in domestic support of agriculture away from those practices with the largest potential to affect production and, therefore, to affect trade flows. However, significant reductions in most agricultural tariffs will have to await a future round of negotiations.

Tariffs, Incentives, and Subsidies

Prior to Uruguay Round, trade in many agricultural products was unaffected by the tariff cuts that were made for industrial products in previous rounds. In the Uruguay Round, participating countries agreed to convert all nontariff agricultural trade barriers to tariffs (a process called "tarification") and to reduce them. However, agricultural tariffs remain very high for some products in some countries, limiting the trade benefits to be derived from the new rules. To ensure that historical trade levels were maintained and to create some new trade opportunities where trade had been largely precluded by policies, countries instituted tariff-rate quotas. A tariff-rate quota applies a lower tariff to imports below a certain quantitative limit (quota) and permits a higher tariff on imported goods after the quota has been reached.

The Agreement on Agriculture required countries to reduce outlays on domestic polices that provide direct economic incentives to producers to increase resource use or production. All WTO member countries are meeting their commitments to reduce these outlays, and most countries reduced this type of support, by more than the required amount. However, support from those domestic policies considered to have the least effect on production, such as domestic food aid, has increased from 1986-88 levels.

In the Agreement on Agriculture, 25 countries that employed export subsidies agreed to reduce the volume and value of their subsidised exports over a specified implementation period. To date, most of these countries have met their commitments, although some have found ways to circumvent them. The European Union (EU) is by far the largest user of export subsidies, accounting for 84 per cent of subsidy outlays of the 25 countries in 1995 and 1996. Despite substantial progress in reducing export subsidies, rising world grain supplies and falling world grain prices will make it difficult for some countries to meet future commitments unless they adopt policy changes.

The Uruguay Round's SPS agreement imposed disciplines on the use of measures to protect human, animal, and plant life and health from foreign pests, diseases, and contaminants. The agreement can be credited with increasing the transparency of countries SPS regulations and providing improved means for settling SPS-related trade disputes, including some important cases involving agricultural products. The agreement has also spurred regulatory reforms in some countries. The SPS agreement and the Agreement on Technical'Barriers to Trade could provide a framework for disputes over genetically Modified Organisms (GMOs) brought to the WTO for arbitration.

Current Issues

Changes made to the multilateral dispute resolution process in the Uruguay Round may be as important to agricultural trade as the improvement in the substantive rules governing trade in agricultural goods. Initial evidence indicates that the WTO dispute settlement system is a significant improvement over its GATT predecessor. For example, a single country can no longer block the formation of a dispute resolution panel or veto an adverse ruling by blocking the adoption of a panel report. These improvements have led to a number of important agricultural trade cases being adjudicated before the WTO. The outstanding question for the WTO is whether members whose practices have been successfully challenged under the new dispute settlement procedures will live up to their obligations.

Other agriculture-related issues, including a bid for membership by a large and diverse group of potential new

WTO members, the challenge of dealing with State Trading Enterprises (STEs) within WTO disciplines, and issues particular to developing countries, will shape the agenda for future agricultural trade liberalisation discussions. Thirty countries are currently seeking membership in the 134-member WTO. Countries seeking WTO membership accede under conditions negotiated with WTO membership through the privileged trade status with WTO member but may incur adjustment costs in reforming their trade policies and reducing tariffs to meet WTO requirements. Current WTO members gain greater access to the markets of acceding countries.

State trading enterprises, governmental and non-governmental entities that have been granted special rights or privileges through which they can influence trade, continue to be important to the trade of agricultural commodities because many countries consider them to be an appropriate means to meet domestic agricultural policy objectives. Continuing concerns about the trade practices of state trading enterprises in some WTO member countries and the potential accession of China and other countries where STEs are prominent will keep STEs on the WTO agenda.

Developing countries received special treatment in the Uruguay Round, including less stringent disciplines in reforming their trade policies than those apply to developed countries. In the next round of multilateral agricultural trade negotiations, developing countries will continue to have their own interests in the areas of special and differential treatment, export restraints, price stability, food security, food aid, and stock policies. As developing countries identify their positions, coalitions of countries with common trade interests may emerge.

Developing Countries and the WTO Agricultural Negotiations

Developing countries as a group have much to gain from continued progress toward a transparent, rule-based trading system in agriculture. The researchers say the negotiations should eliminate export subsidies, impose stricter disciplines on export taxes, cut tariffs, and ensure that food aid continues to be available to poor countries in grant form and delivered so as not to displace domestic production in the countries receiving it. Badly managed food aid, or cheap food imports due to export subsidies, may just reinforce the bias of economic policies against the rural sector. With its negative impact on poor agricultural producers, they say. International research organisations (such as IFPRI, among other institutions) may provide support to developing countries through programmes of collaborative research, technical assistance, and capacity strengthening.

Starting with the first round of trade negotiations under the General Agreement on Tariffs and Trade (GATT) after World War II, there has been a relatively steady trend of increasing multilateral trade liberalisation. The successive rounds of negotiations recognised the greater needs of developing countries, especially since the Tokyo Round. Yet the participation of developing countries was limited. Since many developing countries were not members of GATT, the major forum for airing their views was provided by the United Nations Conference on Trade and Development. The views of developing countries had some impact on the Lome agreements and on aid flows, but had limited influence on negotiations concerning trading rules, which were discussed within the framework of the GATT, where OECD (Organisation for Economic Cooperation and Development) countries set the agenda.

In the Uruguay Round, which began in 1986 and concluded in 1993, developing countries played a larger role in the negotiations compared to previous rounds. In particular, agricultural net exporters organised the Cairns Group (which in addition to Australia, New Zealand and Canada, included several large developing countries such as Argentina, Brazil, Indonesia, and the Philippines) to pursue their interests. Furthermore, during and after the conclusion of the Uruguay Round, the formal accession of developing countries to the GATT and now the World Trade Organisation (WTO) has continued apace. Of the 134 members of the WTO in February 1999, some 70 per cent were developing countries. The United Nations classified 48 countries as least-developed (LLDCs). Within that group, 29 are members of the WTO, six are in the process of accession, and three are observers. Also, 18 countries have been identified as net-food importing developing countries (NFIDCs).

Some Definitions

The LLDCs are identified by the United Nations General Assembly based on several criteria—income per capita, augmented physical quality of life index, and an index of economic diversification. As a group, they have a population of about 590 million people, with an income per capita about 4 per cent that of the world average (1996). Agricultural production per capita in LLDCs has been declining since the 1970s although the same indicator for all developing countries (mainly under the influence of China) has gone up by nearly 40 per cent in the same period. LLDCs represent a small fraction of world trade (less than one per cent for total and about two per cent for agricultural trade). They had a positive, although declining net agricultural trade balance until the mid-1980s, when it turned negative. Almost 20 per cent of their total imports are food items.

The 18 net-food importing developing countries have been selected through a process within the WTO. They have a population of some 380 million people and an income per capita nearly five times that of the LLDC average, but still much lower than the world average. NFIDCs are a diverse group: four are upper-middle income countries; eight are lower-middle income; and six are lower income. Four of them had net food exports on average during 1995-97, but because they imported cereals they are included in the group. NFIDCs' per capita food production as share of both world and developing country averages has risen, although from very low levels.

Although the categories of "developed" and "developing" countries have important legal consequences under WTO rules, there are no formal definitions of either category. The process works through self-identification and negotiation with other member countries of the WTO.

Completing the Unfinished Agenda

In general, developing countries operate under what has been called "special and differential treatment". They face lower disciplines and enjoy longer time frames for implementing reforms. In the case of LLDCs, they are totally exempted from WTO commitments, and it has been agreed that developing and least-developed countries should receive special consideration for market access and technical and financial support. Also, during the Uruguay Round, concerns that liberalisation of agricultural policies and trade could adversely affect the food imports of LLDCs and NFIDCs led participants to include several measures dealing with food security issues in the "green box" of permitted domestic support, for instance, the formation of public stockholding and the provision of foodstuffs at subsidised prices. There was a ministerial decision in Marrakesh in April 1994 to deal with possible negative effects of agricultural trade reforms on the food security of LLDCs and NFIDCs. The decision was reemphasised at the 1996 ministerial meeting of the WTO in Singapore.

Export and Domestic Subsidies

While many developing countries have significantly reduced distorting domestic agricultural policies, the possible benefits that these countries and the world can enjoy are thwarted by the subsidies of developed countries. The Uruguay Round was a first step in imposing discipline on the unfair competition arising from subsidised agricultural exports, which hurts poor agricultural producers in developing countries irrespective of their net agricultural trade position. In the next negotiations, that first step should be completed with the elimination of export subsidies. Net-food importing developing countries should also be interested in stricter disciplines on export taxes and controls that exacerbate price fluctuations in world markets.

Under the Uruguay Round agreement, there is still a lot of scope for the developed countries to use domestic subsidies, in addition to the use of export subsidies; to help their farmers. The developing countries should seek further disciplines in this regard, including, among other things, the elimination of exemptions under the "blue box" (which allows farmers to receive some forms of direct payments that are considered to be trade distorting). Least-developed and developing countries, however, will still be allowed "special and differential treatment" on these issues.

Market Access

If the developing countries are to succeed in diversifying their agricultural sectors, they need expanded access to markets in developed countries. This includes increasing the volume of imports allowed under the current regime of tariff-rate quotas (TRQs, which replaced the previous system of rigid quotas with a combination of a quantitative quota and a high tariff for the eventual out-of-quota imports); making the administration of the TRQs more transparent and equitable; seeking further reductions in tariffs, particularly those still high in some key products; and completing the process of tariffication in the cases where exemptions were granted. Also, eliminating, or at least reducing, tariff escalation in non-agricultural products is important for developing countries: this practice undermines the possibilities of expanding production and exports of processed goods that use agricultural inputs, exploiting "forward linkages" in the value-added chain.

What the Most Vulnerable Need

The special situation and concerns of least-developed countries and net-food importing countries were recognised in a ministerial decision agreed upon at the completion of the Uruguay Round in 1993. These concerns include the preservation of adequate levels of food aid, the provision of technical assistance and financial support to develop the agricultural sector in those countries, and the continuation and expansion of financial facilities to help with structural adjustment and short-term difficulties in financing food imports. It is important to make food-aid available in grant form, to target it to poor countries and social groups, and to deliver it in ways that do not displace domestic production in the countries receiving it. Badly managed food aid, or cheap food imports due to export subsidies, may just reinforce the bias of economic policies against the rural sector, with its negative impact on poor agricultural producers.

Volatility in agricultural prices must be monitored carefully. While expansion of world agricultural trade should limit overall fluctuations by spreading supply and demand shocks over larger areas, the decline in world public stocks as a percentage of consumption works in the opposite direction. Improving early warning of potential food shortages, lowering costs for food transportation and storage, and providing better targeted food aid programmes and financial facilities for emergencies are also issues that need to be addressed by countries participating in the coming round of negotiations.

The impact of changes in trade and agricultural policy on poorer consumers and producers in developing countries is a matter of debate. Some have argued that trade liberalisation may hurt both groups. Others have answered that greater productivity and growth coming from better trade and sectoral policies should help generate employment and income, given a setting of adequate overall economic policies and properly functioning markets and social institutions.

Small producers will also be helped by the disciplines that the URAA is bringing subsidised and dumped exports, while it allows the implementation of a variety of programmes aimed at poor producers or consumers, including stocks for food security purposes and domestic food aid for populations in need. The issue here is the adequate design and funding of domestic policies to achieve the intended objectives of agricultural growth and poverty alleviation, which most certainly will not be helped by trade-distorting interventions either in developed or developing countries.

In general, low-income developing countries and LLDCs should emphasise to the international community the importance of creating and expanding a supportive international trade and financial environment and of implementing an integrated framework for economic and social development, with agricultural and trade polices being an integral part of the strategy. Appropriate measures would include—in addition to the agricultural trade issues suggested here—the continuation and enhancement of the reduction of the external debt of Heavily Indebted Poor Countries (the HIPC initiative) and the further liberalisation of trade in textiles.

But improved international conditions should go hand-in-hand with a better domestic framework in developing and least-developed countries, including stable macro-economic policies, open and effective markets, good governance, the rule of law, a vibrant civil society, and programmes and investments that expand opportunities for all, with special consideration for poor and disadvantaged groups.

Bringing Developing Countries into the Process

Developing countries, as small players in the global arena, should be interested and active participants in the design and implementation of international rules that limit the ability of larger countries to resort to unilateral action. Also, domestic legal and institutional frameworks in developing countries may be strengthened by the implementation of internationally negotiated rules that limit the scope for rent seeking and arbitrary projectionist measures. The developing countries as a group have much to gain from continued progress toward a transparent, rule-based, trading system in agriculture.

What are the requirements and skills for the developing countries to become effective members in the next WTO round? Any negotiation requires careful consideration of the legal, economic, and political dimensions that define the substance and possible evolution of the negotiations, as well as the diplomatic and negotiating techniques that may help in the attainment of the expected outcomes. Questions that need to be addressed include:

- What are the economic and social consequences of different WTO scenarios (quantitative estimation of impacts)? Knowing the impacts of alternative scenarios is crucial if developing countries are to represent their interests in the negotiation process.

- What are the legal issues being discussed (definition of obligations, exemptions, time frame, and so on)? Detailed knowledge of international trade law is crucial if developing countries are not to be "shortchanged." The devil is in the details.

- Looking at the political process, who are the main actors and their interests and what type of alliances may drive the negotiations? Negotiators must understand the political economy of their own country and of other countries in the WTO if they are to negotiate effectively.

- With these elements, an adequate diplomatic and negotiating strategy must be defined and implemented.

Developing countries that have carefully considered all four components will be better prepared to participate effectively in the coming negotiations. Of course, limited financial and human resources act as an important constraint. However, developing countries may overcome some of the problems through collective action, for instance considering the creation of alliances with respect to their main export and import commodities and the markets they approach for their exports. An example is the Cairns Group. This approach could reduce the fixed costs of negotiations. Spreading them over groups of countries, allow a better use of scarce technical expertise, and improve the bargaining position of developing countries. It could also be in the interest of the OECD countries to deal with negotiating blocs, which represent a smaller number of negotiating positions, rather than with numerous separate countries. The negotiations would be much more efficient and balanced.

WTO Agricultural Negotiations

Completing the Task

The Cairns Group of 15 agricultural-exporting countries was formed in 1986 to influence agricultural negotiations within the World Trade Organisation (WTO). It was largely as a result of the group's efforts that a framework for reform in farm products trade was established in the Uruguay Round and agriculture was for the first time subject to global trade liberalising rules. The group is positioning itself to play an important role in the new round of WTO agricultural negotiations.

The Cairns Group, which accounts for about 20 per cent of world agricultural exports, includes both developed and developing countries across a diverse set of regions around the world. The group consists of Argentina, Australia, Brazil, Canada, Chile, Colombia, Fiji, Indonesia, Malaysia, New Zealand, Paraguay, Philippines, South Africa, Thailand, and Uruguay. By acting collectively, this disperate group has had more influence and impact on the agriculture negotiations than individual members would have had independently. Under Australian leadership, the group takes a consensual approach to decision-making.

Beyond the Uruguay Round

Members of the Cairns Group were generally pleased with the Uruguay Round outcome, but believe much remains to be done to ensure that a genuine market-oriented approach to agricultural policies is achieved. For example, in 1997 levels of agricultural support in Organisation for Economic Cooperation and Development (OECD) countries alone were still extremely high at $280 billion. The approach taken by the group to the challenge of reducing this assistance and creating a freer agricultural marketplace has been in two parts. First, the group has worked to ensure that countries meet the commitments that were agreed to in the agricultural-related agreements during the Uruguay Round. It has done this by remaining visible and active since the end of the round.

Second, the Cairns Group has been effective in engaging other WTO member countries in early preparation for the next round of agricultural negotiations in an attempt to ensure that they start on time and are not unnecessarily protracted as they were during the Uruguay Round. The Cairns Group in April 1998 agreed on a strongly worded "vision statement" conveying the Group's ambition and broad objectives for the 1999 agriculture negotiations and initiated a strategic approach to the preparations for the negotiations. This approach is necessarily ambitious. "The Cairns Group of Agricultural Fair Traders reaffirms its commitment to achieving a fair and market-oriented agricultural trading system as sought by the Agreement on Agriculture. To this end, the Cairns Group is united in its resolve to ensure that the next WTO agriculture negotiations achieve fundamental reform which will put trade in agricultural goods on the same basis as trade in other goods. All trade-distorting subsidies must be eliminated and market access must be substantially improved so that agricultural trade can proceed on the basis of market forces."

Objectives for Negotiations

The vision statement outlines the Cairns Group's reform goals in three key areas within the Uruguay Round framework, as follows:

- Deep cuts to all tariffs are required, as well as the removal of tariff speaks and the redressing of tariff escalation so that market access for agricultural commodities and value-added agricultural products is on a similar footing as trade in other commercially traded products. This should include the objective of transforming market access barriers to tariffs and removal of non-tariff barriers to trade. In the interim, the Cairns Group supports substantial increases in trade volumes under tariff-rate quotas, while the administration of tariff-rate quotas must not diminish the size and value of market access opportunities, particularly in products of special interest to developing countries.

- All trade-distorting domestic supports must be eliminated or replaced with non-trade distorting methods of assistance. Income aids or other domestic support measures should be targeted, transparent, and fully decoupled so that they do not distort production and trade.
- Export subsidies must be made illegal for agricultural products, as they are for other traded goods, and clear rules must be established to prevent circumvention of export subsidy commitments. In this regard, it is worth noting that only 25 of the 134 current WTO members are entitled to use export subsidies, and most of these are developed countries (with more than 80 per cent of export subsidies accounted for by the European Union). Also, agricultural export credits must be brought under effective international discipline with a view to ending government subsidisation of such credits.

Special Needs of Developing Countries

The vision statement also reaffirms the group's support for the principle of special and differential treatment for developing countries, including least-developed countries and small states, remaining an integral part of the next WTO agriculture negotiations. The Cairns Group ministers agreed that the framework for liberalisation must continue to support the economic development needs, including technical assistance requirements, of these WTO members. As has been stated by the Cairns Group: Major challenges facing many developing countries are the persistence of rural poverty and the linkages between such poverty and serious environmental problems. Consequently, more sustainable agricultural development remains a central policy issue in many developing countries. An improved international trading environment that is more conductive to supporting agricultural development is needed as an essential ingredient in addressing these problems.

Adherence to these principles will not only improve the trading environment for agricultural exporting nations, but will also have important implications for global food security. Food security will be enhanced through more diversified and reliable sources of supply, as more farmers, including poorer farmers in developing countries, are able to respond to market forces and new income-generating opportunities, without the burden of competition from heavily subsidised products. To provide further assurance to net-food importing countries, export restrictions must not be allowed to disrupt the supply of food to world markets.

Reductions in assistance to the agricultural sector may also have positive implications for the environment. In many cases, agricultural subsidies and access restrictions have stimulated farm practices that are harmful to the environment. Reform of these policies can contribute to the development of environmentally sustainable agriculture.

Preparations for the Next Round

Cairns Group ministers welcomed the launch by the second WTO Ministerial Conference in Geneva in May 1998 of preparations for the next round of agriculture negotiations. The WTO Ministerial Declaration that emanated from this conference binds WTO members to a preparatory process that began in September 1998 and will culminate in ministerial agreement on a decision on the scope, structure, and time-frame for the agriculture negotiations.

The Cairns Group reaffirms its commitment to achieving a fair and market-oriented agricultural trading system as sought by the Agreement on Agriculture. To this end, the Cairns Group is united in its resolve to ensure that the next WTO agriculture negotiations achieve fundamental reform that will place trade in agricultural goods on the same basis as trade in other goods.

28

Opening Markets for Agriculture

While the Uruguay Round made a good start—more was done to liberalize agricultural trade and to bring agriculture into the system than in all previous rounds combined—we have to recognise that agriculture still has a long way to go to complete its reform and to be fully integrated into the world trading system. Prior to the Uruguay Round, agricultural trading rules were not in concert with other sectors. The Uruguay Round Agreement (URAA) made good first step toward bringing agriculture into conformity with international trade rules governing other goods, but much remains to be done.

The Uruguay Round, of course, required certain reductions in trade-distorting measures, and the implementation of those reforms has proceeded very well. Two other legacies of the Uruguay Round are very important for the new negotiations—a mandate to continue what was begun, and a structure for achieving liberalisation. The WTO's "built-in" agenda includes agriculture. It was recognised from the outset that the first period of reform that we are still implementing was only a down payment.

In addition to the commitment to continue negotiations, the URAA—focusing on export subsidies, market access, and domestic support—established a structure on which to build. Establishing a three-pillar structure was the most time-consuming undertaking in the round. Fortunately, we do not need to reinvent that wheel. The structure of the rules provides a logical approach for the negotiations, one which most seem to agree we should keep and build on.

Export Competition

Export subsidies are an illegitimate policy instrument, a symptom of a systemic imbalance in a nation's agricultural policies, the costs of which are borne by others. The costs of domestic policy choices should be borne by the country that chooses them, not foisted onto its trading partners by subsidising exports. The Uruguay Round made a start at eliminating agricultural export subsidies: 36 per cent reduction of budget expenditures on export subsidies and 21 per cent reduction of quantities over a six-year implementation period. With experience to show that markets adapt, we should now be able to improve the pace of export subsidy reductions and eliminate the export subsidy scourge from agricultural trade. Export subsidies are not allowed in the WTO rules for any other industry. Their use constitutes a source of trade distortion and degradation to the environment, and there is no valid reason to keep them any longer.

Market Access

The Uruguay Round progress on market access leaves much to be done. It left tariffs too high, and it did not create much new market access. The average non-agricultural tariff is now 4 per cent, while the average agricultural tariff is over 40 per cent, and tariffs on some products exceed 300 per cent. With a few exceptions, non-tariff barriers were converted to tariffs, and members were required to open up at least a small minimum access—3 per cent of domestic consumption initially, growing to 5 per cent by the end of the adjustment period—under tariff-rate quotas.

The stage has been set for real reforms. Let access continue to grow and let all tariffs be reduced to a negotiated maximum level by the end of the transition period. In addition, an examination of the administration of tariff-rate quotas should lead to transparent and open systems.

Many WTO members note that importers were required to change non-tariff barriers to tariffs and grant access, while no reciprocal disciplines were imposed on export restraints of exporting countries. Net-food importing countries should be able to expect that if they open their border to international market, those international markets will deliver supplies as reliably to importers as to the domestic markets of exporters. Willingness on the part of leading exporting members to discipline export controls will reassure "food security" countries that expanding market access is not risky.

Domestic Support

The Aggregate Measure of Support was a success as a component of the Agreement on Agriculture and the insistence on reducing trade-distorting measures. The drive toward decoupled support ("green box") is the key. By the end of 1996, the United States had largely decoupled farm programmes so that payments to farmers were not linked to a requirement to produce. Other WTO members will also succeed in orienting their policies toward market signals. In the new round, further review and decreases in the aggregate measure of support will clearly lead to market-based agricultural trade.

A new buzzword that some countries are using to justify domestic support is "multi functionality". It is a buzzword for what everybody in agriculture has known for thousands of years: agriculture serves other purposes besides producing food and fibre. But the real problem with the discussion of multi-functionality is not semantic. It is the confusion between policy goals and policy instruments. If the United States appears skeptical about the implications of multi-functionality for WTO rules, the U.S. objection is not multi-functionality as a factual matter. Each country chooses social objectives for themselves. There is no inherent connection between those objectives and trade distorting agricultural policies.

New Issues

While the Uruguay Round established effective disciplines in traditional problem areas, such disciplines have not yet been established in some new areas. As monopolies, state trading enterprises (STEs) can distort trade, and they frequently operate behind a veil of secrecy. The agricultural trading system has much to gain from WTO disciplines on STEs because they allow some countries to undercut exports based on open market transactions and restrict imports.

Biotechnology holds tremendous promise globally for food consumers, producers, and the environment. With the world's population growing by about 2 per cent annually, there are 80 million more mouths to feed each year. Some countries threaten to adopt policies regarding the importation and planting of bio-engineered crops and the labelling of products containing bio-engineered foods that are not based on scientifically justified principles. If our farmers are to meet the challenge of feeding an ever-increasing population with a sustainable agricultural system, then they must have access to the new bio-engineered varieties. We need to think about how the WTO can help facilitate this new technology.

Developing Countries

One of the critical components to a successful new round of negotiations will be the full participation of a substantially increased number of developing countries. Open trade in agriculture relieves farmers in developing countries of the burden imposed by protectionism and export subsidies, while reducing hunger and offering reliable supplies of food at reasonable prices.

29

The Future of Agricultural Trade

In the Uruguay Round, countries recognised that the long-term solution for agriculture did not lie in administered prices, trade restrictions, supply controls, and export subsidies but rather in open, non-distorted markets. It is the time to take bold steps towards bringing agricultural trade into the 21st century by accelerating agricultural trade reform.

There are four key areas for accelerating reforms: eliminating export subsidies; increasing market access through substantial tariff cuts and expansion of tariff-rate quotas; cutting further trade-distorting domestic subsidies; and ensuring technical standards are based on sound science.

The world's farmers and ranchers are facing two difficult challenges at the dawn of the 21st century. First, they are being asked to provide more products at lower cost, higher quality, greater variety, and in a safer manner than ever demanded before. Second, they are being asked to produce this abundance on a shrinking natural resources base that is often subject to government regulations. Meeting these global challenges will require unleashing the production potential of world agriculture while practising proper environmental stewardship. The ingenuity and hardwork we usually associate with farmers will be essential to meet these challenges, but they will not be sufficient unless we further reform agricultural trade to create an environment that rewards risk and investment, and encourages efficiencies.

Today's Agricultural Challenges

Farmers are responsible for feeding a rapidly growing world population. And despite progress over the years, too many people still are not getting enough food. Many countries including the United States, are working vigorously to promote technological innovations to meet the need for food and fiber in the coming years. However, as important as this work is, it is only part of the solution. These technologies and the hard work of the world's farmers need a trading environment that encourages investment and efficient production, and generates economic growth to finance production and consumption needs long-term trends in agriculture pose serious challenges for all farmers. The same technological advances that increase yields may result in lower prices. Increasing social concerns about effect of agricultural production on the environment and living conditions result in new restrictions on farm activities. As urban dwellers and industry stake competing claims for land, water, and energy, many producers find their ability to farm made ever more difficult.

Two approaches to organising the agricultural economy present a stark contrast in dealing with these challenges. One model, popular in Europe and Asia, is to retain an inward-looking agricultural system focussed on supply control and government regulation geared to keeping farm prices high and, since guaranteed high prices are a drain on the treasury, to controlling production. Under this approach, bureaucrats try to assess the optimal level of national production—not so little that imports are needed and not so much that excess production must be bought at high prices and then dumped on world markets. This "command-and-control" structure stifles farmer efficiency and ingenuity and distorts world markets, especially as subsidised surpluses are regularly exported; and it does not address the challenge to farmers to produce food for the next century. It also ignores the interest of domestic consumers (who have to pay high internal prices) and producers in other countries (who have to compete with subsidised products). Of biggest concern is that the anti-market policies of this approach hamstring the agriculture sector from pursuing the technological advances needed to meet its future challenges.

Another approach is to place agriculture on a more market-oriented basis, particularly by removing trade barriers and reducing trade-distorting policies. Greater market orientation was the principle that actions agreed to in the last set of multilateral trade negotiations. In the Uruguay Round, countries recognised that the long-term solution for agriculture did not lie in administered prices, trade restrictions, supply controls, and export subsidies but rather in open, non-distorted markets. Now is the time to take bold steps towards bringing agricultural trade into the 21st century by accelerating agricultural trade reform.

The Gains from Trade

The benefit from free and fair trading of agricultural products have immediate effects on people. Eliminating trade barriers and reducing unfair competition will help ensure that farmers have incentives to produce and consumers have access to the products they desire. Liberalising agricultural trade will contribute to better resource allocation by farmers, which has conservation benefits, rewards low-cost producers, encourages efficiencies, and removes the drag on economic growth.

Opening trading opportunities also increases the food security of food-importing countries by giving supplier countries the confidence required to put more land into production and to create marketing relationships. Trade provides consumers with year-round access to a greater variety of less expensive products, while rewarding producers who are able to find and meet specific consumer demands for high-value products. In a broader context, by allowing imports that are more efficiently produced elsewhere, trade encourages specialisation in efficient agricultural and non-agricultural production.

More dramatically, trade literally saves lives. Without the international flow of food products from areas with abundant production to areas where food is scarce, many people in the world would be eating less or not at all. Trade has dynamic effects, as well, that push long-term productivity growth. For example, access to customers in overseas markets creates an incentive for technological innovation, resulting in exciting developments in improved seed varieties and production techniques. International markets also expand market outlets, raising prices and giving producers increased confidence to produce more than required merely for national needs, allowing productive farmers to not only feed their neighbours but literally feed the world.

Equally important, trade in agricultural products is becoming increasingly critical to farm and ranch incomes. Increased productivity and often times flat domestic demand increases the importance of reliable international markets. Foreign markets are not just a dumping ground for surplus products; overseas consumers value choice and quality, particularly when producers in their own country cannot meet their demands or when they are charged inflated prices. Consequently foreign and value-added agricultural producers, raising farm-gate prices and helping support the range of agriculture-related industries.

Political reality also encourages a focus on international markets: policies based on high government guaranteed prices are ultimately politically untenable because they are hugely expensive, unresponsive to the needs of customers and producers, insensitive to environmental and agronomic realities, and a shameful waste of economic assets. Rather than farming government programmes, our producers are looking for customers around the world.

While agricultural trade benefits consumers and producers alike, it is an area in which progressive reform is ardently opposed by entrenched domestic interests. Producers in some countries, cosseted by high guaranteed prices and protective tariffs, oppose any move toward greater market-orientation. Intervention in the agricultural economy—measured by the Organisation for Economic Cooperation and Development by summing price supports, direct payments, and other support as a per cent of total agricultural production—has actually increased in some countries from the levels at the beginning of the Uruguay Round. In the last set of multilateral trade negotiations, countries began the process of dismantling protection and delinking farm support from production decisions. Consequently, reforms have been undertaken by some countries.

The WTO Opportunity

The major objective in the upcoming farm talks is to accelerate the reform process initiated in the Uruguay Round. That means further substantial negotiations on tariffs, subsidies, and other trade-distorting measures so that the level and direction of trade are determined by market forces, not government intervention. Four key areas are outlined below:

(i) ***Export Competition:*** Export subsidies are the most distorting trade tool because the level and direction of trade is directly determined by government subsidies. Today, the European Union (EU) is the only substantial export subsidizer—nearly all other countries agreed not to use, or have only limited resource to use, export subsidies in the last round of negotiations. EU farmers, responding to domestic prices frequently twice the world price, produce more products than can be consumed in Europe, but at such high prices that they can be sold abroad only with generous subsidies. These subsidies push other competitive suppliers out of the market (which is expensive and unfair) and discourage production in countries that have a comparative advantage in agricultural production (which is wasteful and is threatening both to the environment and to future farm production needs).

In the Uruguay Round negotiations, countries acknowledged the corrosive nature of subsidies and agreed to cap and reduce their use. The upcoming negotiations should eliminate them to ensure that countries do not resort to other policy tools that allow government spending to determine winners in the marketplace. Specifically, WTO members should look closely at curbing distorting state trading agricultural export monopolies that can disguise subsidies and exert distorting market power, along with other policies used to dispose of surplus commodities on a non-market basis.

(ii) Market Access: Measures applied at the border to stop trade currently are the principal barrier to a freer and more open trading environment for agriculture. Market access barriers deny efficient producers the chance to compete in other markets and limit the variety and quality of products available to consumers. Opening markets and maximising trade opportunities as fundamental principles of WTO, and we still have a long way to go in agriculture to open markets to competition.

The Uruguay Round Agreement set agricultural trade on a more predictable basis by requiring that all non-tariff measures, such as quotas and import bans, be converted to simple tariffs. While this was a necessary first step to removing trade barriers, many of the tariffs are still prohibitively high. For example, while the average tariff assessed by the United States on agricultural products is less than 5 per cent (and nearly zero for industrial products), the average agriculture tariff-rate quota (TRQ). Where only specific quantities of imports receive low duties. Many other commodities also are subject to high tariffs.

As we start the next century, higher tariffs should not stop the flow of imported agricultural products. Where TRQs remain as a transitional step before we achieve more open trade, we expect more specific disciplines on the way in which they are administered. Similarly, we need to take a hard look at agricultural state trading monopoly. Importers' use of these state traders may have been justifiable when more restrictions allowed on farm trade, but in the tariff only regime it is hard to see why a government needs to insert itself between an exports and an end-user.

(iii) ***Domestic Subsidies:*** Domestic subsidy programmes are often the root cause of other-distorting policies. Subsidy policies that increase domestic prices above world price levels can be maintained only if price-competitive imports are restricted. Additionally, overproduction generated by high domestic prices can be sold on world markets only with export subsidies that bring the price down to the world price. While reining in distortive domestic subsidy programmes has value in its own right for rationalising agricultural production, the WTO negotiations will focus on their trade-distorting elements.

In the Uruguay Round negotiations, countries agreed to distinguish trade-distorting subsidies (generally those linked to the production of a specific crop or related to price supports) from non-trade distorting subsidies (such as research and development, training and environmental production). The trade-distorting subsidies were capped, and the process of reducing allowable levels of subsidies began. This distinction is a good one: the nasty sort of subsidy that distorts markets and straitjackets producers should be cut, while programmes that will increase a country's ability to produce agricultural products in the next century without distorting production incentives should not be reduced.

(iv) ***Standards:*** As WTO members make progress on cutting tariffs and subsidies, the temptation increase to disguise trade barriers as health and safety measures or other innocuous-sounding "technical standards". Moreover, when regulations purportedly designed to protect health are instead vehicles for domestic protectionism, the credibility of the entire safety apparatus of a country is put up for questioning. When good science is replaced by politics, the basis for sound

health policy is undermined. Therefore, increasing government accountability by putting the emphasis on sound science for health standards should discipline disguised barriers to trade and strengthen health policy.

In the Uruguay Round, countries agreed to a set of sound principles: each has the right to maintain health and safety measures, but these must be based on sound science, backed by scientific evidence and an assessment of the risk, and be no more trade-restrictive than required to meet health goals. In practice, countries have found that these principles work well—bogus measures adopted without scientific basis have been successfully challenged in the WTO without sacrificing health concerns. Creating a supportive environment for the propagation of yield-enhancing biotech products also is critical for meeting the needs of the coming century.

Agriculture is Different

Agriculture occupies a special place in the national economies of most countries around the world. Farmers are responsible for feeding and clothing people. Farming also holds a powerful claim on our national cultures that calls for the preservation of rural lifestyles and values. Farm production is subject to the cruel vagaries of whether and the relentless decline in prices and increases in costs. Some people point to these factors as justifying a different treatment for agriculture in the international economy, including justifying trade-distorting agricultural policies. This is wrong-headed; societies can support farms and preserve rural communities in ways that foster choice, protect natural resources, and expand trade.

Farm production in the next century cannot afford to be trapped in a static system in which prices are determined by government mandate, production decisions are controlled by central planners, and farmers are forced to produce only for local consumers. This myopic system cannot be sustained in any important agriculture producing society. Moreover, this type of system will not meet the needs of the coming century, when we will face unprecedented consumer demand and natural resource constraints.

Instead, I look forward to dynamic world of agricultural trade in which producers, exporters, and retailers apply the creativity of the human mind to the natural bounty of the earth. In this "new" world, we will produce a greater amount and variety of food than ever before, feed the coming billions, sustain our environment, and unlock economic resources otherwise stifled by moribund protectionism, ultimately raising living standards around the world.

30

Export Subsidies

A Distortion to Free Trade in Agriculture

Export subsidies are generally considered one of the most distorting trade tools used by governments to interfere with commercial markets. Export subsidies allow a government to determine the level and direction of trade solely on the basis of government subsidies, lowering world prices and denying sales for other, more competitive exporters. Not only are export subsidies unfair commercial tools, but, by encouraging surplus production, they encourage adverse environmental practices, waste government budgets, and may delay restructuring and reform of domestic industries. Substantial progress toward eliminating export subsidies will be a critical element of the World Trade Organisation (WTO) negotiations scheduled to begin at the end of this year.

The Situation Today

Under the Uruguay Round Agreement, countries agreed to strictly limit the use of export subsidies. First, products that had not benefited from export subsidies in the past were banned from receiving them in the future. Second, where countries had provided export subsidies in the past, their future use was capped and gradually reduced over 6 to 10 years. (Developed countries were required to cut their spending on export subsidies by 36 per cent over six years while also reducing subsidised export quantities by at least 21 per cent on a commodity-specific basis. Developing countries have until 2005 to cut spending by 24 per cent and subsidised quantities by 14 per cent).

Third, countries agreed not to create new schemes that serve as disguised subsidies to get around the product-specific limits. Finally, countries recognised that export credit and food-aid programmes were different and exempted them from the new budget and quantity limits, although there was agreement to negotiate disciplines on export credit programmes to ensure that they do not undermine WTO commitments.

Today, the European Union (EU) is the primary export subsidiser—accounting for nearly 85 per cent of the world total. Nearly all other countries agreed in the last round of negotiations not to use or to have only limited recourse to use export subsidies. EU farmers, responding to domestic prices that are often twice the world price, produce more products than can be consumed in Europe, but at such high prices that they can be sold abroad only with generous subsidies. These subsidies force other competitors out of the market and discourage production in countries with comparative advantage.

If the EU's extravagant domestic subsidies are the root cause of export subsidies, they are also putting serious pressure on the whole EU system. The need to impose budgetary discipline on EU farm programmes (annual cost, about $46 billion) is becoming increasingly evident, even in Europe, and the EU's goal of expanding its membership to new countries is putting pressure on it to bring its farm programmes into line with other countries, which will help reduce its need to rely on export subsidies in the future.

Areas for Resolution

The upcoming negotiations should continue the work begun in the Uruguay Round and eliminate existing export subsidies. There is no economic justification for their continued use. By removing subsidised exports, world prices should increase, and farmers, particularly in the EU, will not be artificially encouraged to overproduce products that they cannot grow competitively.

In addition to eliminating export subsidies, countries should examine the rules defining export subsidies to ensure that countries do not resort to other policy tools that might allow governments to distort markets. Specially, WTO members should to look closely at curbing agricultural state trading export monopolies that can exert undue market power or dispose of surplus commodies on a non-market basis. A recent WTO victory by the United States and New Zealand over Canada's special-class system of dairy exports shows that the existing rule against circumvention are effective but must be enforced.

Export credit and food-aid programmes were addressed in the Uruguay Round agreement in recognition of the fact that those tools could be disguised as subsidies. These policies may again be on the agenda when the WTO negotiations commence next time. It will be important to ensure that the world's needy continue to have access to imported products, even when financial turmoil rolls world markets and limits the ability of developing countries to meet their food and fiber needs.

Certain large exporting nations—primarily in the EU have used export taxes as a supply management tool by intervening in the market to restrict exports when domestic stocks are low. These measures can wreak havoc in international markets, exacerbating price swings and reducing the confidence of net-food importing countries to abandon trade barriers and rely on the international market to provide food security. Similarly, some exporting countries use differential export taxes to discourage exports of basic products (such as grains or oilseeds); they force exporters to process the product domestically (into flour or oil and meal, for example) and export the value added products.

Give Developing Countries A More Favourable Deal

An Assessment of the World Trade Conference in Doha

At the end of the 4th WTO Ministerial Conference in Doha, Qatar, the representatives of all WTO member states vigorously applauded Director-General Mike Moore when he dubbed the adopted work programmes for the new round of trade negotiations the "Doha development agenda."

The launching of a new round of trade negotiations with a broad agenda was the objective persistently pursued by the industrial countries, in particular the European Union, the United States, Canada and Japan. This objective has been achieved. Besides the continuation of the negotiations in the fields of agriculture and services, the Ministerial Declaration adopted by the Conference provides for the opening of negotiations in eleven additional fields. Undoubtedly a success for the industrial countries.

Clear Mandate for a New Development Round

The negotiating mandate, though, clearly reflects the political will to make the new round a "development round" with the aim of significantly improving the integration of the developing countries into the world trading system. To a large extent it takes into account the specific interests of the developing countries. Certainly a success with which the developing countries can credit themselves. A crucial factor for the course and the successful outcome of the Ministerial

Conference was, without doubt, the active involvement of the developing countries in the preparatory and negotiating process.

Doha Determines Merely the Work Programme for Negotiations

The Ministerial Declaration adopted at the conference merely determines the work programme for the new round of trade negotiations. Three factors contributed decisively to the positive outcome of the Ministerial Conference. There was a broad consensus among the WTO members states that (*i*) a second Seattle-like failure would put the WTO's workability at risk and was to be avoided at all costs (the 3rd WTO Ministerial Conference I Seattle in December 1999 ended in chaos without the adoption of a Ministerial Declaration); (*ii*) the recessionary trends in the world economy were to be countered with the successful conclusion of the Ministerial Conference in Doha to improve the prospect for short-term recovery and, thereafter, sustained economic growth; (*iii*) in response to the terrorist attacks of September 11, 2001, there should be a clear commitment to strengthen the rules-based multilateral trading system. Failure was, therefore, not an option. The strategic conclusion drawn from the Seattle failure was to limit the Doha Ministerial Declaration to establishing a broad, generally-worded negotiating mandate for a new round of trade talks that does not anticipate the outcome of the negotiations on controversial issues. The strategy worked. The deliberations at the Ministerial Conference focussed on the scope of the negotiating mandate. The task of reconciling the conflicting interest between industrial and developing countries and working out a fair compromise has been left to the forthcoming negotiations.

Recognition of the Interests of the Developing Countries

In view of the objective of creating a basis for sustained economic growth in the developing countries by better integrating them into the world economy and increasing their share in world trade, important preliminary decisions with regard to the forthcoming negotiations were taken by the Ministerial Conference:

- The Ministerial Declaration stresses the importance of implementing and interpreting the Agreement on Trade-Related Aspects of Intellectual Property Rights (TRIPS Agreement) in a manner supportive of public health and access to medicines; in recognition of the seriousness of the problem, a separate 'Declaration on the TRIPS Agreement and Public Health' was adopted; a number of public-health related issues have been referred to the Council for TRIPS for further deliberation;
- The Council for TRIPS has been tasked to examine the relationship between *(i)* the TRIPS Agreement and the Convention on Biological Diversity and *(ii)* the protection of traditional knowledge, taking full account of the development dimension;
- Numerous problems regarding the implementation of WTO agreements are dealt with in a separate 'Decision on Implementation-Related Issues and Concerns' adopted by the Ministerial Conference; outstanding implementation issues are to be addressed as a matter of priority by the relevant WTO bodies;
- The Council for Trade in Goods will examine the proposal to bring forward the liberalisation of the textile sector under the Agreement on Textiles and Clothing;
- As regards agriculture, comprehensive negotiations were agreed on, aiming at: substantial improvements in market access; reductions of, with a view to phasing out, all forms of export subsidies; and substantial reductions in trade-distorting domestic support;
- As regards market access for non-agricultural goods, negotiations were agreed on, with the aim of reducing

or, as appropriate, eliminating tariffs and non-tariff trade barriers, in particular on products of export interest to developing countries;

- Recognition of the principle of special and differential treatment of the developing countries as an integral part of all WTO agreements;
- Technical cooperation and capacity building have been recognised in the Ministerial Declaration as 'core elements of the development dimension of the multilateral trading system' and firm commitments have been established in various paragraphs.

Turning the Ministerial Declaration's Spirit into Practical Policy

With these preliminary decisions regarding the agenda of the forthcoming negotiations, the course is set for the better integration of the developing countries into the world economy. To stay the course, there must be clear commitment and political will on the part of the industrial countries to make the new round a 'development round' by taking the developing countries' interest fully into account, being prepared to make meaningful concessions, and making good on the promise of significantly increased trade and investment-related technical assistance.

In the course of the negotiations it might prove a problem that many of the obligations in favour of the developing countries are formulated rather vaguely. The Ministerial Declaration is confined to declarations of intent even where—with a certain degree of goodwill—binding commitments would have been politically feasible. The bringing forward of the liberalisation of the textile sector, a key demand of the developing countries, has been referred to the Council for Trade in Goods for examination; this is certainly an expression of the industrial countries' willingness to compromise, but it in no way anticipates the final decision. As regards the objective of duty-free and quota-free access for all products of the least developed countries to the markets of the industrial countries the Ministerial Declaration simply repeats the commitment which was already expressed in the United Nations Millennium Declaration of September 2000, at the 3rd United Nations Conference on Least Developed Countries in Brussels in May 2001, and at the G7/8 Summit in Genoa in July 2001. Except for the European Union, no party has put this commitment into practice so far; the United States and Japan in particular have shown little enthusiasm for introducing duty-free and quota-free access of all LDC products.

What makes us believe that the Doha Ministerial Declaration will make a difference? The chapter on agriculture is more specific in that it provides for negotiations aimed at significantly improved market access, reductions/phasing out of all forms of export subsidies, and substantial reductions in trade-distorting domestic support. However, a clear road map including a timetable for the negotiations and specific benchmarks for the reduction targets were beyond Doha's reach; in addition, the qualifier that the commitment to comprehensive negotiations does not prejudge the outcome of these negotiations leaves a back door open. In conclusion: If you remove the merely rhetorical phrases—such as "we place the developing countries' needs and interests at the heart of the World Programme adopted in this Declaration", "to take fully into account the development dimension...", —from the Ministerial Declaration, it becomes quite clear that the text contains relatively few 'programming elements' with a view to the development agenda of the forthcoming negotiations.

Fears that the vested interests of the industrial countries will re-gain precedence over development aspects in the course of the negotiating process are certainly not entirely baseless. The 'steel war' the United States is about to declare on the rest of the world clearly indicates that the Doha fair weather period is over. Business as usual has returned. The American steel tariff threats prompted EU Trade Commissioner Pascal Lamy to speak of a "perverse signal at a time when the ink is barely dry on the Doha Agreement."

The non-governmental organisations have a decisive role to play. It is their role to monitor the new round of trade negotiations, to make the negotiating process more transparent, to create public awareness with regard to the issues at stake, and to build up political pressure with the objective of making sure that development aspects are not pushed to one side and that the interest of the developing countries will make their way into the agreements to be concluded.

Coherence of Trade Policy and Development Policy

The negotiating mandate for the new round of trade talks adopted in Doha has brought development politics onto the agenda of the WTO. The mention of development aspects in the WTO set of rules and regulations is not, in essence, new. In fact, the development dimension is recognised as an integral part of the general WTO mandate to foster economic growth. However, the particular importance the Doha Ministerial Declaration attaches to the consideration of development aspects in the negotiation process (it seeks, as it is put there, "to place the developing countries' needs and interests at the heart of the work programme") offers the opportunity to achieve greater coherence of trade policy and development policy. In this respect, the Doha Ministerial Declaration reflects the same trend as the "Everthing-but-Arms-Initiative" (EBA) of the European Union. Subsequent to its adoption by the EU member states, Pascal Lamy emphasised the coherence aspect as the characteristic feature of EBA initiative (outweighing the shortcomings relating to bananas, rice, and sugar) by saying, "It is the first time that the European Union's trade policy has been substantially modified by the necessity of contributing to development policy." This perspective also characterised the 3rd United Nations Conference on Least Developed Countries in Brussels in May 2001.

To sum up, it can be said that the Doha conference has sent out an important signal for the process of coordinating trade and development policy with the long-term objective of achieving a coherent policy framework. The next step towards greater coherency can be taken at the International Conference on Financing for Development in Monterrey/ Mexico in March 2002.

Sustainable Development as the Guideline for Further Developing the Multilateral Trading System

The Ministerial Declaration reaffirms the commitment to the objective of sustainable development, as stated in the preamble to the Marrakesh Agreement of April 1994 (i.e. the Agreement establishing the WTO). However, theory and practice are far apart. The negotiating mandate for the new round is too cautious a step towards integrating environmental and social aspects into the WTO set of rules and regulations to be able to bridge that gap. Looking at the three pillars of the sustainable development concept—economic development, environmental protection, and social protection—, in a nutshell the following can be said:

The negotiating mandate for the new round deserves good grades as far as the first pillar, economic development, is concerned. The course is set for better integration of the developing countries into the multilateral trading system, thus giving them the chance of actually benefiting from further trade liberalisation in the form of trade-induced economic growth. The inclusion of the so-called 'Singapore issues', investment and competition, offers the prospect of a medium to long-term improvement of the business and investment climate in the developing countries. As for environmental protection, negotiations on a (very) limited scale have been agreed on, the desirability of further negotiations will be examined. This is certainly not a big breakthrough, but a first step towards integrating ecological aspects into the trade rules. Disappointingly (but not surprisingly), social issues were not dealt with at the Doha Ministerial Conference. The developing countries' resistance to even discussing social issues, such as core labour standards, in the framework of the WTO could not be overcome; the issue was considered an absolute 'deal-breaker'.

Outlook

The developing countries' consent to the launching of a new round of trade talks cannot disguise the fact that there are still significant differences of opinion over a number of issues, including such key issues as agriculture, environment, investment and competition, and that there is a great deal of mistrust on the part of the developing countries. The one-day extension of the Ministerial Conference alone is proof of how difficult the process of reaching consensus on the launching of a new round of trade talks and its agenda had been. In order to successfully conclude the new round, the industrial countries have to deliver on their commitments, such as improving market access for goods of export interest to the developing countries and increasing their trade-related technical assistance.

The assurance of increased technical assistance was a major bargaining chip in getting the development countries' OK for the new round. If insufficient funds for technical assistance and capacity building measures are provided, it will most certainly diminish the chances of getting quick results. In a comment on the forthcoming negotiations, the British Economist also highlighted the credibility aspect and the need for significant concessions, "Poor countries remain deeply suspicious of the rich world's commitment to truly freer trade. They bitterly remember the Uruguay Round, whose benefits went mostly to the rich. For the new talks to succeed, those suspicions must be proven wrong. Europe and America must quickly open up their markets for farm products and textiles. They must show that environmental concerns are not going to become a backdoor excuse for renewed protectionism. They must reform their oft-abused system of anti-dumping rules. And they must deliver on promises to beef up poorer countries' capacity to deal with the intricate procedures in the world trading system."

The Doha Ministerial Declaration offers the prospect of long-term gains for the developing countries. However, turning potential into actual gains requires tenacity in pursuing policies aimed at improving the business climate and, in general, the framework conditions for economic growth. Increased trade-related technical assistance and improved market access will not automatically result in growing export volumes for the developing countries. In addition, the strengthening and diversification of productive capacity is required. Successful integration into the global economy depends on tackling the supply-side constraints and other 'behind-the border impediments to trade' (ranging from weak infrastructure, insufficient ancillary services and poor governance to macro-economic instability). The Tanzanian Trade Minister, Iddi Simba, emphasised the complexity of the problems the developing countries are facing in his statement at the Ministerial Conference: "To operationalise the development agenda we need to have adequate capacity building which will go beyond addressing the normal WTO obligations. Adequate resources in the form of financial and technology transfer need to be in place to address the supply-side constraints. Along the same lines, WTO Director-General Mike Moore stated, "Capacity problems [in producing goods and services competitively], not trade barriers, are the major obstacles to growth in developing countries."

Concluding Remark

By creating a rules-based multilateral trading system, the WTO set of rules and regulations contributes to the shaping of the process of globalisation and to the emerging system of global governance. However, it can hardly be disputed that so far the industrial countries have been the main beneficiaries of the WTO-driven economic globalisation. We are still miles away from a true win-win situation. In a recent interview with the German weekly *Die Zeit,* the Nigerian President, Olusegun Obasanjo, criticised the industrial countries' hypocrisy, saying "Globalisation is a good thing. But only if there is a level playing field, from which all countries are able to benefit. You tell us that we have to open up our markets for your goods, whereas you keep your markets closed for our goods. Europe protects itself with innumerable trade barriers, everybody knows that. What kind of rules are those?"

That is exactly what matters. The new round of trade negotiations launched in Doha must result in modified trade rules. Trade rules which take account of the specific economic constraints of the developing countries and are more favourable to them. The developing countries must be given the chance to 'cash in' on trade liberalisation and, strengthened by trade-induced economic growth, to pursue national pro-poor policies aimed at eradicating poverty.

32

Can Economic Growth Reduce Poverty?

New Findings on Inequality, Economic Growth and Poverty

Many people still think first of 'economic growth' in relation to poverty reduction. Indeed, their correlation is one of the most-discussed issues of combating poverty. The relationship is of great importance because if there is a clear causal dependency, reducing poverty could fundamentally be limited to measures to promote growth. However, if there was low growth or stagnation if would not be possible to reduce poverty decisively. In the opposite case, that of the phenomena having no causal relation, promising measures to reduce poverty could be taken up even without economic growth.

Hardly anyone now explicitly expresses the view that economic development trickles down automatically to the poor. Practical experience has refuted this assumption dating from the early days of development policy in the 1960s. However, a number of studies show development of growth and a decline in poverty running parallel. On the other hand, there are also examples which show that despite high economic growth, poverty is not reduced markedly. The common answer to the question this raises is thus: Yes, growth can reduce poverty, but only if additional measures oriented on the poor are taken up. This is often termed pro-poor-growth. But what that means in detail, and whether economic growth as such plays a causal role at all, is not clarified. It is worth taking a look at the arguments on the basis of more recent empirical and theoretical knowledge.

No Direct Causality Between Growth and Poverty Reduction

Among the many indicators of poverty, the income of the poor (income poverty) has the closest relationship to economic growth. An increase in gross domestic product and thus national income could, if other factors come into play be linked with an increase in the per capita income of the poor.

Such a relationship between economic growth and the income of the poor, however, cannot be described as causal, as is asserted implicitly time and again by the statement that growth is a necessary but not sufficient precondition for poverty reduction. In so far as growth and poverty reduction arise at the same time at the end of a process, they exist alongside each other. It would be almost a tautology to say that the former is the cause or part-cause of the latter. Both express the same thing, namely a change in per capita income as well, and both have similar causes. What matters is recognising what these causes are and what specific factors must come into play so that the income of the poor grows too. Growth as a "prerequisite" or "condition" is then no longer the focus; the priority is asking for specific policies that result in higher incomes for the poor. The detour in thinking about growth is not necessary. Since, however, it is based on similar factors, such as fiscal policy/ budget structure, employment policy, combating inflation, and institutional development, economic growth can also emerge if poverty is reduced. The difference of views lies in the fact that under the heading 'poverty reduction' the aim is no longer growth, but a purposeful reduction of poverty.

Therefore, in reverse, successful combating of poverty can be seen as being the cause of growth insofar as activating the capabilities of the poor and using their productive capacity triggers economic drive.

Indirect Causality Between Growth and Poverty Reduction?

So even if economic growth fundamentally has no direct causal impact on poverty, growth still can reduce it indirectly. This is the case when due to positive economic development a government has greater revenue and uses the surplus for combating poverty, for example by providing such public goods as education and health services. Also in these cases, however, growth is not a compelling precondition. Even without growth greater government revenue can be achieved for example by more efficient tax collection. And leeway for social welfare spending can be gained by redistributing the budget, such as by cutting military appropriations. Furthermore, an automatic process is not given because the government can also use surplus funds for non-social purposes.

Creation of jobs due to increased economic activity can be another indirect link between economic growth and income poverty, if such a development generates income and reduces poverty. But also in this case I see no compelling causality because, for instance, industrial jobs are not necessarily open to the really poor. In addition, these positive impacts occur to a considerable extent only in the event of labour-intensive development. In many countries, however, economic growth is achieved by capital-intensive production.

Inequality, Growth and Income Poverty

If national incomes, grow, a naïve observer might assume that the income of the poor must also grow along with it. But that would be a statistical fallacy. Even if only the income of the rich grows, this results in macro-economic statistics showing a higher per capita income. What the true conditions are is shown as soon as one divides the population statistically into income groups, such as in fifths, as is usual. It then turns out that the bald figures on average per capita growth can certainly cloak a situation where the income of the richest fifth of the population is growing fast while that of the poorest fifth is stagnating. Despite growth, the gap between the two becomes even wider.

The unequal distribution of income (and of other assets such as property and access to social services), and its connection to poverty reduction and growth has recently returned to the forefront of the debate.

It is obvious that inequality and its changes have direct effects on the poverty situation. Does inequality also have an impact on poverty via its relation to growth, because growth promotes or reduces inequality? Earlier, the predominant view was that rapid growth was linked with at least a temporary increase in inequality, so that a distinct policy of growth initially disadvantaged the poor.

The current dominant view is that growth has no foreseeable effects on inequality and that inequality changes only very slowly, in reverse, however, it is assumed that greater equality is a determinant of growth. According to that view, an indirect relationship between poverty on one side and inequality as a factor dependent upon growth on the other is not given.

That leads to the conclusion that fair distribution has more weight than growth. Fair distribution, however, does not depend upon growth. An appropriate policy is possible at any time, not only after an economic situation has improved. The notion that still shimmers through the debate that "something must be earned first before it can be distributed", is wrong. It is a matter of designing policy and the entire economic process right from the start in such a way that the surplus benefits all including the poor. Important elements of such a policy are, for example, land reform and development of finance systems.

Relationship of Growth to Poverty

According to today's conventional wisdom, income poverty expresses only a part of what poverty means. Not least through the voices of the poor themselves, it has become clear that violation of human dignity and rights, a lack of participation in decisions and exclusion from society, unequal treatment of men and women, and vulnerability are also regarded as poverty. For poverty is caused to a great degree by conflicts of power and interests. Income poverty often is not even seen as the greatest problem.

What relationship do these more far reaching characteristics of poverty have to economic growth? A direct relationship of growth to socially-related aspects such as women's inheritance rights, land rights and exclusion from decisions cannot be seen. Considerable improvements in favour of the poor can be achieved here even without economic growth.

Those who see a strong and causal connection between economic growth and poverty reduction must ask themselves what the prospects are for high growth rates and thus for a decline in poverty. Coupling poverty reduction to economic growth is problematic. If only low growth rates are to be expected.

Another question is whether continuous increases in growth are at all desirable and possible in the medium to long-term. In this connection, a difference should perhaps be made between developing countries and industrialised nations. But environmental compatibility and availability of resources set limits to growth for both. Some academics assume that industrialised nations have already reached an inherent limit (stagnation theory) and that the high growth rates of earlier years will not return. Moreover, they add, full employment is no longer achievable due to, among other things, an ongoing increase in productivity, and current unemployment cannot be reduced by customary means. In any case, if growth were to be taken as the major benchmark, the prospects for a radical reduction of income poverty around the world would be modest.

Summing Up

Poverty is a complex problem and reducing it depends upon many interconnected factors that is why poverty cannot be attributed to one main cause nor its reduction based on one main strategy. Economic growth is just one strategic element among many others related to poverty reduction. An indirect causal connection between growth and poverty reduction can only be seen because governments will have a greater scope for action due to economic growth, and if they promote labour-intensive development.

Therefore growth's role in poverty reduction must be put into perspective. Growth cannot be the first thing that comes to mind, nor is it the golden path to reducing poverty. The simplistic theory of economic growth as the main condition obstructs the bigger picture; it clings to the underlying and ongoing belief in the trickle-down effect. Even if there is no growth or for inherent reasons there can be none, there are promising ways to take on the challenge of mass poverty in the developing countries. Up front, governments and bilateral and multilateral donors must have the political will to design economic, financial and social policies so that they are oriented on poverty in a coherent way—the result can also be economic growth.

33

Challenging Traditional Economic Growth

Today, saving the planet is about redefining our economic development models. Striving towards the fulfilment of basic human rights is an integral part of environmental protection. Without a people-centred development strategy we will fail. Conflicting interests and lack of vision and courage are among the many reasons why it is so hard to meet needs in a world of plenty. We are faced with three major challenges in the 1990s.

- To curb population growth and poverty
- To search for sustainable production and consumption patterns
- To promote equity.

Population growth is often associated with poverty. But who causes the major strain on the environment? The 1.2 billion poorest people consume small amounts of the world's resources and contribute little to harmful emissions. They do not cause a heavy burden. The day-to-day struggle for survival of the poorest does, however, undermine their resources, and this causes deaths as population grows beyond the carrying capacity of nature. Here two key elements are essential: to turn from non-renewable to renewable resources, and to minimize use of resources through resource efficiency. We must single out the products and processes that must be phased out and those which may be allowed to expand. Right prices that include the ecological costs will be explored further, together with administrative measures. We are ready to examine the possibilities of using "geen tax" reforms to enhance employment and harness pollution and inefficient resources use. By shifting the burden of taxes from labour to environmentally harmful products and processes we might achieve a double benefit.

Transport, waste management, energy and land-use are obvious areas that need to be affected by policy changes. Individuals must use their power as green-conscious citizens and shoppers—but, in the end, producers and service providers hold the main key to practical action.

The market must be harnessed to meet people's needs both for present and future generations—starting by making economic policies play by the rules of nature. The World Trade Organisation (WTO) negotiations have provided us with instruments to regulate world trade.

Getting the Prices Right

Car emissions may be cut drastically, but the rapid increase of new cars nullifies the benefits. Even the most ardent technological optimist must admit that we need new priorities or cuts in some products and services. For example, we must improve public transport and resource-efficient cars—and reduce traffic.

Traditional economic growth models fall short of solving the problem of unemployment. Indeed, 'robots' and wasteful resource use replace people. There are great job-creating possibilities in environment-friendly produces and processes. Striving towards equity within and between nations, and within and between generations, is the major challenge of our time.

The fact that 20 per cent of the world's population consumes 80 per cent of the world's resources has too long been seen as mainly an ethical challenge. Ethics are not easily translated into politics, especially when confronted with economic and market realities. As equity gradually becomes a security issue—as it will, if we do not bridge the gaps within and between nations—it will climb to the top of the political agenda.

Many of the main conflict areas of today are battlefields of resource management. These will expand greatly if we do not turn conference statements of good intention into action. The 30 year-old commitment of the rich countries to meet the target of 0.7 per cent of GNP in official Development Assistance remains unmet.

Two hundred years of Western-led development optimism reached its peak in the late 1980s. When the Berlin wall fell, the economic growth models of the rich countries had become the universal recipe. But as more and more people aspire to join the ranks of the middle classes, the resulting environmental stress calls for a halt, or a radical change of course.

The call for new patterns of production and consumption challenges our traditional concepts of economic growth and the focus on materialism in our culture. Neither the industrialised nor the poorer countries are strangers to radical process of change, though the reasons for change are shifting. And we are truly facing challenging and conflict-provoking changes.

No nation by itself can solve the problems we face. Pollution knows no frontiers, but comes to us with the winds and waves. We have become more and more interdependent. If we are to attain sustainable development, we must commit ourselves through international agreements, through an international rule of law, through the development of financial mechanisms and through institutional agreements. We must develop means and tools to enhance collective security and mutual interests.

34

Consuming the Future

Now that we are to reach six billion of us, it is a good point to check again on what sort of lifestyles we pursue and what is the environmental impact of those lifestyles. It is curious that we have spent several decades being concerned about the growing numbers of humankind while not giving at least an equal amount of attention to the levels of living we aspire to, and how many natural resources we chew up thereby and how much population and waste we cause.

Everybody is a consumer of sorts. True, every fifth person scarcely qualifies for that designation, consuming goods worth less than $1 per day. Conversely, every seventh person qualifies for a designation of super-consumer, with a cash income at least fifty times greater. These latter are the people who, through their carbon dioxide emissions, are disrupting everybody's climate dozens of times more than the average citizen of One Earth. Fair Play, anyone?

Much as the have-nots seek to match the have's, it is plain their efforts will not work out for a long time to come, at best. If every Chinese person were to consume just one additional chicken per year and if the said chicken were to be raised primarily on grain, this would account for as much grain per year as all the grain exports of the number two exporter, Canada. If the Chinese were to raise their per-capita consumption of beef, now only 4 kgs per year, to that of Americans, 45 kg, and if the additional beef were produced largely in feedlots after the manner of the United States, it would account for as much extra grain as the entire US grain harvest, less than one-third of which is exported. Because of its recent climbing up the food chain toward a meat-based diet, China has become one of the world's leading importers of grain. The global grain market today is around 200 million tons per year, and shows scant scope for significant increase.

As a further measure of its ambitions, the Chinese government has designated the auto industry as one of five industry "pillars". Today China has fewer cars than Los Angeles. If per-capita car ownership, together with oil consumption, were to match that of the United States, China would need 80 million barrels of oil per day—by contrast with the world's 1996 oil output of 64 million barrels of oil per day. The surge in carbon dioxide emissions would be unprecedented.

All this notwithstanding, there are already some 250 million newly affluent people in China. They are people with a household income equivalent to perhaps US $20,000, and enough discretionary income to enjoy the perquisites of the good life as perceived by these nouveaux riches. Top of the shopping lists are meat and more meat, followed by cars whether big or small. These are the badges of success: they show you have arrived.

The new consumers in China are matched by at least 200 million in India, and tens of millions in South Korea, Taiwan, Malaysia and Thailand (the recent economic setbacks have not permanently punctured the economic bubbles). Then there are 200 million more in Brazil, Argentina, Venezuela and Mexico, and more again in Hungary and other countries of Eastern Europe, also Turkey. Put them all together and they total about as many as the 800 million long established consumers in the ultra rich countries (the OECD grouping). When the current economic hiccups in Asia are left behind, the ranks of the new consumers can be expected to rise rapidly.

But they cannot hope to become super consumers. Where would all the extra grain come from? How could the global climate tolerate the huge additional pulse of carbon dioxide? There are all kinds of other environmental reasons to suppose that environmental constraints will become all the more constraining. True, technology could help moderate the environmental impact. We could enjoy twice as much material prosperity while using only half as much natural resources and causing half as much pollution and waste. But the new consumers will want to pursue the American dream to the hilt, and it is hard to see that the best technologies could enable huge numbers of affluent aspirants, perhaps two billion people by 2010, enjoying even half the material prosperity of Americans with average household incomes of $40,000.

But is it true "prosperity"—mental and emotional as well as material? Or is the American dream becoming a nightmare with its harried lifestyles and declining leisure time, where the shopping mall is the ultimate mecca, and the good life is a case of piling up goodies?

In any case, we cannot expect the new consumers to forego their "rightful share" of affluence unless the long-time affluent agree to cut back on their environmental ruinous lifestyles. It is these communities that must offer a strong example, and soonest. Where is the political leader who will espouse the new vision, however much it may be perceived as the ultimate vote loser?

Development

The People Know Best

Meetings of the World Bank and the World Trade Organisation has inspired high-mined protest and, on occasion, even vandalism. But this protest and vandalism may miss the point. It is hard to blame those who complain of bullying or blundering by the great institutions of global power. But the poor of the world, especially the poor of developing countries, deserve more than street demonstrations. The poor understand better than anybody the complicated details of their own poverty – the absence of health care, the lack of education, and all the sinister perils to their own safety and well-being. They know the failures of their governments, and of international institutions.

And that is the point: It is the people of the poor countries who will have to apply new knowledge to design and achieve their own development. A country can only develop when its citizens have the freedom to address their own development problems. The obligation of the rich countries, is to give help where they can. And anyone who doesn't see a moral imperative to contribute to a fairer, more prosperous future is free to frame the obligation differently—as self-interest, for example. It will surely serve us better to invest in a peaceful and contented global community than to invite the strife and poverty of unanswered injustice and economic ruin.

Among our relevant conclusions: Powerful institutions of global finance and trade (not least, the World Bank and the World Trade Organisation) can be a source of real promise to poor countries. If governed right, they can help integrate developing economies into the enriching opportunities of global trade and investment. But such promise is often wasted because the very poverty of poor-country governments weakens their ability to negotiate the terms that would serve them best.

Communities in poor countries find themselves at a special disadvantage when it comes to bargaining with foreign investors. Investment can bring growth and spread wealth. It can also threaten human rights and social cohesion, or cultural integrity, and the fragile balance of ecosystems. Nobel Economist Amartyasen has spoken powerfully about the intimate relation between development and choice, the subject of his thought-provoking book Development as Freedom. Development, Sen argues, "consists of the removal of various types of unfreedoms that leave people with little choice and little opportunity ... " He defines freedom as "both the primary end and the principal means of development."

A precondition of this freedom is knowledge—knowledge of the hard facts and the hard science, on which real choices are constructed. Also it is knowledge of good governance—procedures of choice that are effective, responsive and democratic. For budgetary reasons, rich countries contribution to international development was severely cut in the 1990s. Now, along with others in the rich countries, they have to begin to reinvest in international development.

This means a new commitment to the improvement of lives, and to the future that the North must share with the South. It will be a reinvestment in peace, and in our own prosperity. This remains a matter of obligation, and of sensible self-interest.

Finance Matters

Financial Liberalisation Too much too soon?

An efficient and stable financial system is important for economic growth and poverty reduction. The financial crises that have afflicted many countries in recent times have been a costly and painful reminder of the disastrous consequences for development of weak financial markets. The recurrence of financial crises, at both the international and national levels, and the adverse effect they have had on economic growth and poverty levels, have highlighted the need for a policy framework which addresses the inherent vulnerability of financial markets to systemic instability and failure.

Governments have always intervened in the financial sector and there are sound theoretical and practical reasons for doing so. Financial markets are characterised by problems of limited and unequal information, making them inherently imperfect and prone to failure. Financial regulation and supervision are therefore essential for efficient and stable financial market development. How should governments intervene? Have financial liberalisation and financial sector reform made financial systems more, or less vulnerable to instability and systemic crises? How can the process be better managed? What is the best policy framework for supporting financial sector development in low-income countries.

Repression to Liberalisation

For many years, governments followed a policy of financial 'repression', which relied on fixing interest rates below market levels and controlling the allocation of credit. The economic distortions induced by these policies were considerable. Financial systems remained under-developed, lending patterns were inefficient and failed to achieve their distributional goals. Negative real interest rates led to low savings and encouraged capital flight. Macro-economic performance also deteriorated countries with large negative real interest rates experienced lower allocation efficiency and growth rates. In the state-owned banking sector, poor lending decisions (often politically influenced) and low repayment rates led to bank insolvency and large budgetary bailouts of depositors and creditors.

A growing awareness of the economic costs of financial 'repression', led to financial 'liberalisation' as the dominant policy paradigm over the past two decades. Initially, the relaxation of controls on interest rates was the focus for financial reform which was often triggered by a financial crisis. The relaxation of controls on the financial sector was often part of a more general policy shift towards liberalisation of the domestic economy and opening out the international economy liberalisation soon broadened therefore beyond interest rate liberalisation, to include a wide range of measures constituting a programme of financial sector reform was adopted under World bank sectoral or structural adjustment lending conditionalities, the key elements of which included privatisation of banks, entry of new domestic and foreign entrants in to the banking sector, bank restructuring and recapitalisation, opening upto the capital account, strengthening bank regulation and supervision institutions.

Has Financial Liberalisation Worked

The period of financial liberalisation conincided with, or was soon followed by heightened financial instability, culminating in the dramatic financial crisis in East Asia in the second half of the 1990s. Clearly, financial liberalisation has not led to a smooth transition to a stable and efficient financial system. It would be wrong, however, to jump to the easy, but shallow, conclusion that financial liberalisation has 'failed'. Firstly, the fat that the period of increased systemic instability does not prove causality. Secondly, no process of change comes cheap: a reasoned assessment of the costs and benefits of the policy change is needed. And thirdly, what would have been the outcome without the policy change". Finally the impact of financial liberalisation will differ between countries, depending on each country's economic and institutional characteristics. The more relevant research issue, therefore, relates to the design and timing of context-specific policy measures, which will contribute to the development of an efficient and stable financial system. Could financial liberalisation have been managed better? If so, what policies are now needed? The commercial banks are the dominant component of the financial sector in low-income countries and are critical to the efficiency and stability of the financial system as a whole. Financial liberalisation was associated with a shift in prudential regulation from direct regulation of banks, by for example, regular site visits, to an indirect approach based on the monitoring of bank capital to ensure that it remained adequate in relation to the risk being taken. Additional regulatory measures are also necessary to restrain the activities of the privatised and other newly-established private banks. The regulatory and supervisory framework may also need to be extended, to cover micro-finance institutions which have developed significant deposit taking capacity.

Four main obstacles to efficient banking regulations are:

(a) Information, contracting and monitoring problems;

(b) Lack of supervisory personnel;

(c) High operational costs; and

(d) Poor credibility and regulation of regulatory bodies. The appropriateness of various policy measures for dealing with these constraints are discussed and ranked in terms of their suitability for low-income countries. What are the implications of allowing micro-finance institutions to offer a range of financing services beyond small-scale lending.

Too Much, Too Soon?

The experience with financial liberalisation reveals a strong correlation between liberalisation and financial crisis. This can be explained partly by the exposure of existing inefficiencies and distortions in the financial structure, and partly by a failure to develop a strong regulatory and supervisory framework, prior to liberalisation. Weakness in the initial conditions affect the ability of the privatised banks and new market entrants, to operate on broadly commercial principles. Borrowers are often unable to service their loans, due to poor quality lending and high interest rates. Liberalisation of the capital account increases the inflow of foreign capital, but at the same time threatens that stability of the financial institutions by increasing the exchange rate and domestic lending risks.

The existing regulatory and supervisory system may be unsuited to a market-based environment. Consequently, across-the-board 'big-bang' financial liberalisation and financial sector reform increase the likelihood of systemic crisis, where the institutional and human resource environment is weak. Much of the blame for post-liberalisation financial crisis lies, therefore, with the scale and sequencing of financial reform. What is needed is a more gradual and considered approach to financial liberalisation, which recognizes that institutional strengthening, especially in the regulation and supervision capacity, is a prerequisite and supervision capacity is a prerequisite for creating a more efficient and stable financial sector which can contribute fully to achieve economic growth and poverty reduction in developing countries.

37

Technological Entrepreneurship

The New Force for Economic Growth

Entrepreneurship has emerged as a major new force for change. The dynamic role of modern small business in economic growth has received fresh recognition worldwide. It is essential to promote entrepreneurship and to mobilise the dynamism of the private sector for accelerated national development. An unbridled private sector may not, however, ensure growth with equity. It is the prime responsibility of governments to create policy frameworks that enable businesses to apply technology for competitive advantage and for the well-being of the public.

The Changing Global Environment

As agents of change and progress, entrepreneurs start by identifying a market opportunity and matching this with social or technical innovations. They then proceed to mobilise the resources necessary to drive their business concept to its commercial realisation. The development of a product or service with a high-technology content—never easy anywhere, or at today's rapidly-changing global environment. It calls for restructuring the available technology and business development systems and developing the skills needed by a new breed of "techno-entrepreneurs" to transform innovations into market opportunities at home and abroad. It also requires reorienting the present processes and priorities of technical and economic cooperation among countries.

Amidst the global concerns of environmental preservation, poverty elimination and social development, the practical problems of entrepreneurship are not being properly addressed, .even though entrepreneurs will create the bulk of enterprises, jobs and wealth.

A torrent of technology-based goods hits the market every week, ostensibly improving the quality of our lives while simultaneously creating complexity and dislocation. The pace of progress in information technologies, micro-electronics, robotics, new materials, biomedical sciences, space science and other advanced technologies quickens, significantly changing the way we live. The growth of markets for these technologies also proceeds apace.

Further, technological change is taking place today against a background of growing intra-national and international disequilibria. While the transformation from state-centred to market-oriented development is opening up enormous opportunities and options, it has also caused severe short-term hardships. In order to survive and prosper in these changing times, India and its enterprises need enlightened government policies, good technical infrastructure and strong cultural roots.

Traditional production factors are giving way to a new paradigm characterised by new patterns of trade, investment and employment, and by informal networking life-long learning and technological entrepreneurship. The manufacturing sector in India continues to be dominated by food products, textiles, chemicals and other traditional industry, mainly in the public sector. However, change is coming, albeit slowly. State enterprises are being corporatised pending privatisation, and the share of knowledge-based and information-related activities in the marketplace is rising perceptibly. Restructuring policies now place emphasis (often purely rhetorical) on the role of the private sector. The legacy of decades of centrally-planned development is generally inimical to private enterprise. In turn, the private sector has been slow to respond to economic liberalisation in India and generally failed to generate the new employment necessary to absorb new entrants to the labour force.

The regulatory problems of an onerous tax structure and administration, poor access to finance and raw materials, over-regulation of labour and land-use, pervasive bureaucracy and restricted markets have been significant barriers to entrepreneurial growth.

Towards Competitive Performance

The imperative of improved performance has serious implications for India if it is to survive, stay abreast and succeed. It calls for national efforts on systemic efficiency and productivity growth, the move from an investment-driven to an innovation-driven economy and sustained higher-order competitiveness; towards enhanced customer satisfaction at home and penetration of selected markets abroad. Concurrently, governments and business have to address such intractable problems as poverty, corruption and the degradation of the environment.

Creating New Technology-based Ventures

Starting a new business in India is a hazardous task. Problems are compounded when the venture is technology-based:

- Capital requirements are generally larger, while traditional banks are ill-equipped to process the perceived risk. Venture capital generally only becomes an option when the venture has documented the merits of its management, market and innovation.
- Knowledge-based ventures can benefit from linkages to sources of knowledge, e.g. the technical university or research lab. Such mentoring needs to be cultivated.
- Techno-entrepreneurs often have technical skills but usually lack the business management and marketing skills necessary for success. These need to be supplemented.

- In fields where technology is changing rapidly, it is often advantageous to make technology-acquisition arrangements. Sourcing such innovations, negotiating technology licensing agreements and protecting the intellectual property itself require special skills.
- Knowledge-based innovations are inherently more risky than others. The management of this unique risk requires assessment techniques and vision.
- Technology-based ventures often have social and environmental implications, which need to be managed carefully.
- Penetrating a competitive market requires good market intelligence, a good strategic plan and good luck.

Special Characteristics of "Techno-entrepreneurs"

The popular misconceptions are that techno-entrepreneurs are born, not made; that they take risks with other people's money and fail more often than they succeed. In fact, entrepreneur skills can be identified and developed. The entrepreneur is typically an innovator who formulates new solutions to existing problems, mobilises resources and stimulates others to participate in his or her team. These aptitudes develop over time, often starting in childhood, as the person faces new challenges and learns from failure.

Entrepreneurial opportunities can be found in every industrialising country, community and family. Principal sources of entrepreneurs for knowledge-based ventures are often the university and government research laboratories, the large industrial and military establishments and professional service firms. Some motivations of the entrepreneur are the need to be independent; create value; contribute to society; earn recognition; become rich or; quite often, simply not to be unemployed. Value-adding ventures with good growth potential can best be developed in an open market and in a culture which supports risk-taking.

The techno-entrepreneur anywhere has the challenge of moving a concept through the prototype and production phases towards creation of a product which meets market needs at a price consistent with the value created and with the ability of customers to pay.

Equally important, the market itself has to be developed and sustained. It is not enough to be first with a better mousetrap if one does not have the skills to educate and reach potential buyers and to set the market standard.

Hence one has to distinguish between innovators and inventors. The inventor is typically a creative person in a quest for knowledge or for producing new products, without determining in advance whether a real market exists for his or her inventions. On the other hand, the innovator draws on existing knowledge and the talents of others to develop or adapt a product or service at a volume and cost that can capture a significant portion of an identified market. The flexibility and creativity of a small entrepreneurial techno-venture may lead to more incremental and break-through innovations than can be generated by larger-sized firms in many sectors.

The pace and pattern of India's economic development now depend in large measure on its technical resource base. In this context, the key determinants are the skills to apply technology for enhanced competitiveness, as well as to create tech-based ventures. Techno-entrepreneurs have to be supported by appropriate national structures and international linkages if they are to survive and flourish in an intensely competitive world.

38

Money Alone is not Enough

Technology Transfer and Environmental Protection

In the seventies it was a hotly debated topic, in the eighties it became a moot issue: The demand of the developing countries for low-cost or even free technology transfers from the industrial nations. The environment, or more accurately, the endangered environment, is responsible for reviving this subject once believed to be dead. Politicians in the South were quick to see the opportunity which presented itself: No environmental protection without technology, no technology without technology transfer, no technology transfer without money.

The Montreal treaty (on the reduction of chlorofluorocarbon production) was an important first step. It established a fund which supports the environmental efforts of the developing countries. But this was only the beginning. Technology was one of the main concerns of the United Nations Conference on Environment and Development (UNCED).

It is undisputed that private enterprises control the expertise necessary for environmentally sound technologies. The discussions in the developing countries revolve around this basic issue: What guarantees are there that these firms will transfer any technologies at all and at an acceptable price to boot? Both premises present a problem: In all likelihood, technology monopolists have invested substantial amounts in the development of the respective technology and will therefore try to sell their licenses at the highest possible price (price problem). Having had so many failures with specific projects in the past, many firms are not quite reluctant to transfer technology to the developing countries. It was no coincidence that North-South technology transfers practically came to a standstill in the eighties.

Technology cannot be purchased as a package. This is a frequently forgotten truism. By general definition, technology consists of four components:

- Hardware, for instance a specific configuration of machines and equipment to manufacture a product or provide a service;
- Know-how, i.e. scientific and technical knowledge, qualifications, and empirical knowledge;
- Organisation, i.e. the arrangement which combines hardware, know-how, and operational management methods;
- The end product, i.e. the item or service.

The technical components (machines, blueprints) and products (licenses) can be purchased subject to the cited restrictions, but not organisation and qualifications. This is the real bottleneck for technological development in most developing countries. There is not inductive to the process which is most important for the utilisation of technology technological learning.

The core of technological knowledge is the mastery and subsequent continuous improvement of production processes. In part this happens automatically (learning by doing), but beyond that it must be actively stimulated. Many examples in both industrial and developing countries show that firms frequently stagnate at a certain technological level, thus missing a chance to improve efficiency. The main reason is inadequate technological knowledge. The secret of optimizing the conversion process lies in a strategy of small steps, the steady improvement of individual segments.

The economically most dynamic developing countries are successful because of high productivity increases made possible by technological competence, i.e. the ability to assess and evaluate the technology offer, to select, utilize, and improve technologies, and ultimately develop new ones. This latest state-of-the art processes can be used for industrial expansion projects. As far as these countries are concerned, the introduction of financing mechanisms for the transfer of environmentally sound technologies represents a very promising approach.

Technological Competence the Crucial Factor

In other countries industrialisation efforts have caused serious environmental degradation but little economic development. The reason is last but not least inadequate, only slowly growing technological competence. Those countries have hardly any money to invest in environmentally sound technologies. But even if the international community establishes financing mechanism, the problem of inadequate technological competence remains unsolved. It is unreasonable to assume that in a country, where conventional production technologies are used ineffectively and inefficiently, environmentally sound technologies can suddenly be applied in a meaningful and efficient manner. For these countries the transfer of environmentally sound technologies is a "quick fix" which in all likelihood will not work. Without an established level of national technological competence, it will not do much good to shower a country with technology from outside (more precisely, with technical hardware and production know-how).

This brings us to an original development policy problem. Technology and technology transfer have always played a big role in development policy, although quite often the perspective was short-term: Instead of technology, only hardware was transferred; frequently, technological competence was not developed in the recipient countries, but rather substituted with external experts. In the future, much more emphasis will have to be placed on stimulating the technological learning process and promoting national technological competence. Many developing countries have already moved in this direction, such as instituting macro-political reforms, which pressure private industry to increase performance, thus forcing technological learning. But development policy can make a contribution as well. Above all, it will have to adopt a more systemic approach and promote structural improvements at several levels:

- As a systemic link between project and project environment. Technology institutions have always been the darling of environmental policy, but frequently they had too little contact with potential users and therefore remained ineffective.
- As linkage with indigenous efforts in the recipient countries and with the activities of other donors. Isolated projects and competition among donors are a guarantee for failure. On the other hand, the fascination in many recipient countries with individual technologies is slowly being replaced by a growing understanding of the technological correlations, concerted technological political actions, which have already been initiated in some developing countries (for instance Thailand, Jordan and Tanzania) and which brought together representatives of government, private industry, educational and research institutions at "round table" discussions, provide an opportunity for the systemic incorporation of technologically oriented development policy measures.

A Dual Challenge for the Industrial Nations

The industrial nations are thus faced with a dual challenge. First, they must support those developing countries financially whose technological competence is adequate for the effective utilisation of environmentally sound technologies. On a global scale, this is an ecologically rewarding undertaking. Since environmental standards have been low in these countries, investments can achieve substantially higher reductions of pollutants than in the industrialised North. There is another aspect: The industrial nations can put pressure on the developing countries to use environmentally sound processes only if they simultaneously offer financial compensation. Secondly, the industrial nations must increase their efforts to raise the level of technological competence in developing countries. This is an essential pre-condition for the developing countries to be able to participate in the medium term in an environmentally benign growth model.

39

The Truth About Global Competition

The Economic Myths Behind Globalisation

Local communities everywhere are on the front lines of what might well be characterised as World War III. It is not the nuclear confrontation between East and West—between the Soviet Union and the United States—that we once feared. It is a very different kind of conflict. There is no clash of competing military forces and the struggle is not defined by national borders. But it does involve an often violent struggle for control of physical resources and territory that is destroying lives and communities at every hand. It is a struggle between the forces and institutions of economic globalisation and the communities that are trying to reclaim control of their economic lives. It is a conflict between competing goals—economic growth to maximize profits for absentee owners versus creating healthy communities that are good places for people to live. It is a competition for the control of markets and resources between global corporations and financial markets on the one hand and locally owned businesses serving local markets on the other.

Two things of fundamental importance to each and every one of us are now very much at stake.

- Will people and communities control their local resources and economies and be able to set their own goals and priorities based on their own values and aspiration? Or will these decisions be left to global financial markets and corporations that are blind to all values save one—instant financial returns?

- Will the life sustaining resources produced by the regenerative capacities of our planet's ecosystems be equitably shared to provide for the material needs of all of us who inhabit this bountiful planet, as well as for our children and their children unto the seventh generation and beyond? Or will we allow a global economic system that is now functioning on auto-pilot beyond conscious human control to consume and destroy the ecosystem and our social fabric in its insatiable quest for money?

Economists, politicians, corporate spokespersons and the media have for years been touting the benefits of the global economy. They have called on us to support trade agreements such as the North American Free Trade Agreement (NAFTA) and the World Trade Organisation (WTO) to remove the constraints of economic borders and open to everyone the opportunities of growth and prosperity in the global economy. They have promised rich rewards for those workers and communities that become successful global competitors.

Many of the most ardent boosters of economic globalisation met earlier in the year at the annual meeting of the World Economic Forum. This Forum has for years brought together top industrialists and political figures from around the world to advance the proposition that removing tariffs and other restrictions on the free international flow of trade and money is a key to creating new economic opportunity and prosperity. It thus caused quite a stir when the Forum publicly announced that economic globalisation is producing disastrous consequences that threaten the political stability of the Western democracies. Their warning bears close examination for being one of the most honest and accurate assessments of the consequences of economic globalisation yet produced by leading advocates of that process. The observation is that:

- Economic globalisation is causing severe economic dislocation and social instability.

- The technological changes of the past few years have eliminated more jobs than they have created.
- The global competition "that is part and parcel of globalisation leads to winner-take-all situations; those who come out on top win big, and the losers lose even bigger."
- Higher profits no longer mean more job security and better wages. "Globalisation tends to delink the fate of the corporation from the fate of its employees."
- Unless serious corrective action is taken soon, the backlash could destabilize the Western democracies.

We don't have to go far to find examples of what they are talking about and why people are getting a bit upset as they wake up to the realities of who is winning in the ruthless competition of the global economy. The disparities between the winners and losers in the global competition are becoming more obscene with each passing day.

We are coming to realize that the extravagant promises of the advocates of the global economy are based on a number of myths that have become so deeply embedded in Western industrial culture that we have grown to accept them without examination.

- The myth that growth in GNP is a valid measure of human well being and progress.
- The myth that free unregulated markets efficiently allocate a society's resources.
- The myth that growth in trade benefits ordinary people
- The myth that global corporations are benevolent institutions that if freed from governmental interference will provide a clean environment for all and good jobs for the poor.
- The myth that absentee investors create local prosperity.

The Growth Myth

Our measures of growth are deeply flawed in that they are purely measures of activity in the monetised economy. Expanded use of cigarettes and alcohol increases economic output both as a direct consequence of their consumption and because of the related increase in health care needs. The need to clean up oil spills generates economic activity. Gun sales to minors generate economic activity. A divorce generates both lawyers fees and the need to buy or rent and outfit a new home increasing real estate brokerage fees and retail sales. It is now well documented that in number of other countries the quality of living of ordinary people has been declining as aggregate economic output increases.

The growth myth has another serious flaw. Since 1950, the world's economic output has increased 5 to 7 times. That growth has already increased the human burden on the planet's regenerative systems—its soils, air, water, fisheries, and forestry systems—beyond what the planet can sustain. Continuing to press for economic growth beyond the planet's sustainable limits does two things. It accelerates the rate of breakdown of the earth's regenerative systems—as we see so dramatically demonstrated in the case of many ocean fisheries, and it intensifies the competition between rich and poor for the resource base that remains.

This is vividly illustrated by many of the development projects in India many funded with loans from the World Bank and other multilateral development banks—that displace the poor so that the lands and waters on which they depend for their livelihood can be converted to uses that generate higher economic returns—meaning converted to use by people who can pay more than those who are displaced.

The Myth of Free Unregulated Markets

It is almost inherent in the nature of markets that their efficient function depends on the presence of a strong government to set a framework of rules for their operation.

We know that free markets create monopolies, which government must break up to maintain the conditions of competition on which market function depends.

We also know that markets only allocate efficiently when prices reflect the full and true costs of production. Yet in the absence of governmental regulation, market incentives persistently push firms to cut corners on safety, pay workers less than a living wages, and dump untreated toxic discharges into a convenient river. In our present competitive context if management does not take such measures, they are likely to be replaced by the owners or bought out by someone with less scruples who will.

The Myth of Free Trade

Many so-called trade agreements, such as the North American Free Trade Agreement (NAFTA) and the World Trade Organisation (WTO) are not really trade agreements at all. They are economic integration agreements intended to guarantee the rights of global corporations to move both goods and investments wherever they wish—free from public interference and accountability. WTO is best described as a bill of rights for global corporations.

The Myth that Economic Globalisation is Inevitable

Many of the people who claim globalisation is a consequence of inevitable historical forces are paid to promote that message by the same global corporations that have invested millions of dollars in advancing the globalisation policy agenda.

The Myth that Corporations are Benevolent Institutions

The corporation is an institutional invention specifically and internationally created to concentrate control over economic resources while shielding those who hold the resulting power from liability for the consequences of its use. The more national economies become integrated into a seamless global economy, the further corporate power extends beyond the reach of any state and the less accountable it becomes to any human interest or institution other than a global financial system that is now best described as a gigantic legal gambling casino.

All over the world people are indeed waking up to the truth about economic globalisation and are taking steps to reclaim and rebuild their local economies. Such communities face basic choices as to how they will divide their efforts between competing for a share of the declining pool of good jobs that global corporations offer and working to create locally owned enterprises that sustainably harvest and process local resources to produce the jobs and the goods and services that local people need to live healthy, happy, and fulfilling lives in balance with the environment.

Our experience with the real consequences of economic globalisation is pointing to many important lessons. One such lesson is that economies should be local, rooting power in the people and communities who realize their well-being depends on the health and vitality of their local ecosystem. If it is protectionist to favour local firms and workers who pay local taxes, live by local rules, respect and nurture the local ecosystems, compete fairly in local markets, and contribute to community life—then let us all proudly proclaim ourselves to be protectionist.

Such choices are not isolationist. To the contrary, they create a foundation for creative cooperation with our neighbours—whether they be in the United States or in other countries—to share experience, ideas, and technology—and to join in international solidarity in rewriting the rules of the global economy to favour local over global businesses, and to encourage cooperative relations among people and communities. It is our consciousness—our ways of thinking and our sense of membership in a larger community—not our economies—that should be global.

Millions of people are also making an important discovery—that life is about living—not consuming. A life of material sufficiency can be filled with social, cultural, intellectual, and spiritual abundance that place no burden on the planet.

It is time to assume responsibility for creating a new human future of just and sustainable communities freed from the myth that greed, competition, and mindless consumption are paths to individual and collective fulfillment. It will take millions of people around the world—linked together into a powerful political coalition aimed at radical, political and economic—reform to win the war that global capital is waging against us.

40

The Dematerialisation of the World Economy

The first Industrial Revolution marked the transition from robber-and-plunder colonialism to the systematic development of the "overseas" territories in the framework of the international division of labour between raw materials suppliers and manufacturers of finished goods. There was an "historic integration" of the colonised areas in the development of their parent-states. What will the third Industrial Revolution do for the Third World? Will it now come to an "historic separation"?

The end of the East-West conflict was reason enough to talk about a radical change in world politics. But at the same time an upheaval in the world economy is taking place that possibly will have even wider impacts. As a reference point for the following thoughts, three dimensions of this change are pointed out:

1 The upgrading of processing information rather than materials as object of economic activity (technological dimension);

2 The evolvement of global communications networks (socio-cultural dimension);

3 The change of the nature of work (socio-economic dimension).

All three dimensions can be summarised under the buzzphrase "tertialisation of the world economy."

In that respect, talk of the "Third Industrial Revolution" is misleading. It is not about a third epoch of industrialisation, but about the beginning of a de-industrialisation, the transition from the industrial to the information society.

Historic Separation?

In the 1960s and early 1970s, there was often talk of the Third World as the Third Sector of the world economy. Also then the Third World was not much more than an "imaginary community". But as such it had a certain significance in world politics. This implied not only its strategic role in the East-West conflict and its ideological function as the supporter of different "third paths" between capitalism and socialism. It was also about the Third World's attested "chaos power". That linked the fear (in the North) and the hope (in the South) that the developing countries would be in a position to cut off the industrial nations from supplies of important raw materials, thus putting them under pressure. But it was soon seen that both sides had over estimated this possibility, even with regard to oil. Instead of supply bottlenecks arising, raw materials prices plummeted. For some commodities, the fall in prices exceeded those of the Great Depression of 1929/30.

This was due, inter alia, to the conjunction of lower demand from the industrial nations and expansion of production by the raw materials suppliers. Business activities dependent upon the supply of raw materials are tending to lose importance compared with the overall development of the global economy. The reason for this is to be seen in the transition from a material to an information economy.

This transition is taking place in line with the revolutionising of data transmission and the expansion of financial transactions which are not directly related to changes in the production of materials. The speed of the changes is remarkable.

However, the dematerialisation of business activities does not lead to decoupling of the Third World from the world economy. Declining market shares in world trade are not the expression of separation, but a loss of the affected countries positions in the world economy. Thus, the impact of dematerialisation is "only" that the negotiating positions of raw materials suppliers vis–a–vis the industrial nations will deteriorate further.

Differentiation of the Third World

But the radical change in the global economy is affecting some developing countries worse than others. Sub-saharan Africa, and some countries in West and South Asia and Latin America are being pushed back further. The oil-producing countries with their high per capita export earnings will be able to hold their positions in the world economy for some time to come. The threshold countries of East and Southeast Asia can expand theirs so long as they can continue to attract a growing share of global industrial production, and at the same time participate in the tertialisation of the world economy in the shape of rapidly-growing financial transactions. Thereby it should be noted that the degree of tertialisation in itself is not an adequate indicator for economic avant-gardism. Brazil exhibits a high degree of tertialisation in combination with a low macro-economic development dynamics. A good part of its tertialisation is being achieved by speculative financial transactions with their inherently greater risks and uncertainties than in the industrial countries. Such dangers have been demonstrated by Mexico's peso crisis and its repercussions on the whole of Latin America.

In some Third World countries, a "location annuity" has replaced the old raw materials one. Here it's about providing locations for off-shore transactions which offer international capital traders a maximum of freedom of movement combined with low taxation. Suitable for such operations are small countries which, despite low levy rates, achieve significant income in macro-economic terms.

The radical changes in the world economy are spurring the differentiation of the Third World without, however, necessarily fostering a dissolution of the Third World as an "imaginary community". It is precisely the advanced countries of East and Southeast Asia that are showing a certain interest in the formulation of joint positions of the "South" in order to secure their own positional gains in the global economy. It's not by chance that the non-aligned countries and the Group of 77 have formed a joint coordination committee, and that the ASEAN countries are changing course on the international human rights policy.

Hitherto, the developing countries' strategy was to broaden the concept of human rights as a justification for demands on the industrial nations. But of late some developing countries, led by the ASEAN states, have questioned the universal validity of human rights even after their universality was confirmed by consensus at the Conference on Human Rights in Vienna in 1993. Playing a role in this policy is the governments' fear that due to the expansion of global communications networks, the behaviour patterns and preferences of their own people could in some way become similar to those of the West. As the rulers see it, that would be detrimental to the continuation of the development models practised so far.

Internet Creates New Cultural Dimension

Much information which Asian governments view as subversive in already globally available on the Internet. The old struggle over the world information order, which at first was primarily a clinch between East and West, is thus taking on a new dimension. For with the growing importance of computer literacy to a country's ability to assert itself on world markets, the Asian threshold countries have not only an interest in controlling the on-line communication but also to expand it and the know-how that it requires.

Even the critics of any interventions in the internet and other global communications networks must admit that modern communications technologies are politically blind and their use in itself does not represent progress. The setting up and expansion of global information highways will offer forum not only to people who want to use it for education and enlightenment, but also to all shades of fundamentalists. These highways will not necessarily bring the misery of many Third World regions closer to the industrial countries, but possibly rather strengthen the tendency to process all world events as entertainment.

Global Two-thirds Society

The gravest aspect of the current upheaval in the world economy is its negative impact on jobs. The information economy needs for fewer workers than an economy based on materials. Instead, the demands on the skills of the workers are growing. Twenty per cent of the world workforce will in future be employed as (overworked) "intelligence workers". Eighty per cent will work parttime, if they are not underemployed or jobless. So the tertialisation of the global economy delivers more underemployment rather than more leisure time. The workers who are rationalised out of their jobs in the industrial sector cannot be absorbed by the service sector because it, too, is not left untouched by rationalisation measures. The civil service is also cutting back on staff. At all levels, there's a race to make the greatest possible savings on payrolls. At the same time, there's growing pressure to cut costs in providing for the victims of this development. That means thinning out the social security safety net.

The bottom line is that the two-thirds society, which developmental action groups hitherto assumed was limited to the Third World, is spreading worldwide. That, however, will not in the foreseeable future lead to an amendment of the North-South disparities. It is true that the change in the global economy is taking place faster, and to a greater extent in the industrial nations. But rationalisation is also happening in the developing countries in a bid to boost their competitiveness. So the upheaval in the world economy aggravates the problems which exist in a majority of the developing countries, while creating new ones in the industrial nations. The need for action on the North-South policy is growing, while the industrial nations' scope for concessions and compromises is shrinking. The new social question which is now crystallizing at global level is not being answered. The consequences are unforeseeable.

Another Loser?

It is more probable that a sharpening of the North–South confrontation is to be reckoned with. The industrial nations will attempt to keep the social costs of the information economy at bay for as long as possible. The trade unions will thereby compete with the developing countries for jobs for their members. But this policy has its limits precisely because of the peaking of the problems in the industrial nations. Overstepping these limits means war, and passively accepting them chaos and social decay. Solutions could be sought in two directions: effective taxation of the information economies, and the creation of jobs in the non-profit sector. But it is possible there are no global solutions for global problems. That would mean for at least part of the Third World a renewal of the old debate on partial decoupling from the world economy.

41

Using Economics to Advantage

In the eyes of the public, the economic sectors—for instance energy, transport and agriculture—are often seen as pursuing interests that conflict with environment and health. They are the originators of pollution and often devise economic arguments to oppose changes in their practice that could improve environment and health. This behaviour has led the public, as well as environment and health professionals, to view economic analysis negatively. However, these economic arguments are often inadequate and unconvincing from the point of view of many economists.

In fact, the economic rationale is bound to reflect as closely as possible the preferences of the population and thus to take much greater account of environment and health. If used by environment and health authorities, economic analysis can be turned into a powerful tool for supporting their policies.

Why Use Economics?

First, economics can help to make explicit the benefits of environmental health improvements and the costs of the impacts. This provides additional arguments to encourage decision-makers to integrate environment and health considerations in their policies.

Second, current prices rarely reflect the full environment and health costs of the production or consumption of goods and services. Therefore, producers and customers have no economic reasons to reduce the impact they have on environment and health, as they do not pay prices that reflect this impact. Nor are they encouraged to take it into account in their investment decisions and lifestyle choices.

This could be corrected by reflecting as much as possible environment and health costs in the prices. Economic instruments, such as environmental taxes or tradable permits are a promising solution. A first step in that direction is the removal of subsidies that support practices harmful to the environment and health. In most of the cases, however, it would be difficult to remove decorative subsidies immediately and charge the full amount of environment and health costs. Nevertheless, negotiating plans and timetable to do so progressively, is a strong signal to the economic actors. It modifies their anticipation of future prices, as they know they will have to pay in the future for the environment and health costs they will create. This drives them increasingly to design their long-term choices and strategies in an environment-friendly way.

Finally, the setting of new economic instruments is usually under the responsibility of the Ministry of Finance. It also implies negotiations with economic sectors. Therefore environment and health authorities will need to play a more pro-active role in order to advance the integration of environmental health in sectoral and economic policies. Success will depend on their ability to discuss and present economic arguments in support of environmental health considerations.

A Promising Initiative

The present situation is that many environment and health authorities have few skills in using economic arguments and that economic sectors very often continue to ignore environment and health considerations.

International organisations—will also be invited to strengthen their co-operation in environment and health economics. In order to sustain the policy changes, promoting environment and health, co-operative efforts will aim.

- To support the development of the capacities of the environment and health authorities to use economic analysis;
- To improve the focus on health outcomes in national or inter-country processes dealing with environment and health issues. This will include the contribution of health expertise in these processes and the use of economic arguments to greater advantage;
- To exchange information early in the planning process of their respective programmes that use economic tools for addressing environment and health;
- To further co-ordinate their current and future activities in support of environment and health.

Beyond Economics

Unless policy-makers take a more all-round view of education, they risk sending their countries down the wrong path. Over the past decade, educational change in most countries has been driven by one imperative: survival in the global economy. This process has been particularly salient in the Asia-Pacific region following the drastic shock of the 1997 economic downturn. But in the current reform process, marked by speeding commercialisation and economic preoccupations, other educational missions are being ignored, and countries risk paying a high price for their short-sightedness.

There's no denying that economic considerations are critical in today's world. Students have to acquire the knowledge and skills to survive and compete in the global economy, especially one which more than ever before prizes human capital. A high-quality labour force gives nations a cutting edge in global competition. Understandably, stressing economic returns in the current educational debate attracts private resources. But education has other functions that are the indispensable corollary of more balanced, equitable development. They deserve to be briefly explained.

The first is a social function: education has a role to play in facilitating social mobility and bringing about integration in often very diverse constituencies. It is at school that children learn how to form a broader set of relationships, to live together and become aware of belonging to teach us civic attitudes, to make us aware of our rights and responsibilities—in essence, to become responsible citizens. The task is fundamental in light of democracy's advance in so many countries over the past decade or so. Then there is education's cultural function. Developing creativity and aesthetic awareness, accepting other traditions and belief systems while valuing our own are all part of the path towards fulfilment. Finally, education is a goal in and of itself. Schools help children learn how to learn and play a pivotal role in transferring knowledge from one generation to the next. I believe that all these facets of learning are critical for the long-term prosperity of our societies. In our globalised, interdependent world, these functions take on a more international character. Everywhere, education has a role to play in eliminating racial and gender biases, promoting global common interests, moments for peace, and greater international understanding.

Rising Above Short-term Pressures to Strike a Harmonious Balance

While education is widely recognised as the spine of the learning society, the complexity lies in striking a balance between these various functions. The commercialisation of education that we are witnessing the world over inevitably pushes schools, educators, parents and policymakers to pursue short-term, market-driven outcomes. Lawyers, bankers and businessmen have an increasingly high profile in educational debates. Following Southeast Asia's downturn in 1997, they were influential in changing the academic mindset. In little time, emphasis has shifted from academic achievement to developing communication skills, creativity, adaptability. In and of itself this is not necessarily regrettable. The problem is that these skills are all perceived to be at the service of a supreme economic value.

Sounder research will be required to analyse and assess where the current trends are leading us. It is increasingly recognised, however, that unless economic growth is accompanied by good governance, a fair sharing of benefits, better social and environmental protection and attention to culture, it will, sooner or later, lead to unrest. It is through education that this broad spectrum of concerns can be nurtured. Policymakers who have taken stock of this holistic mission unfortunately represent a minority in today's educational debates and reforms. Their foremost challenge is to manage commercialisation, to rise above short-term pressures and to take a more ethical stance towards education, a long-term strategic view.

43

Consumption Bomb

It is three decades since we passed the peak world population growth rate of 2.04 per cent. Annual additions too are now a decade past their peak of 86 million a year. They are currently running at 78 million a year and are heading downwards. A peak in total numbers, however, still lies at least four or five decades ahead. On the UN Population Division's 1998 projections, the total is likely to reach 8.9 billion in 2050. The long range medium projection, which has not been updated since 1996, expects world population to level out at just under 11 billion in 2200 AD.

However, this is based on assumptions that are increasingly questionable. More and more countries are reaching levels of female fertility that are not enough for replacement—below 2.1 children over the lifetime of each women. At the latest count there are 61 countries in this category. Of this 23 had very low fertility, below 1.5.

The situation is unprecedented in times of global peace on economic growth. The UN medium projection assumes that where fertility is very low it will rise again to 1.7-1.9 children per woman. In all countries where fertility is currently above replacement level of 2.1, it assumes that it will not fall below that level.

Yet fertility has fallen below replacement level in so many countries, which such different cultures and different stages of economic growth, that is increasingly looking as if low fertility may be here to stay. If this became the case, then world population may peak at somewhere between 8 and 9 billion. Thereafter it may well begin to decline. The 1996 long range low projection has world population falling to 5.6 billion in 2100 AD.

None of this means that reproductive rights should have lower priority in future. Their contribution to the health and welfare of women and children is clear. Many poor countries in Africa and South Asia face huge population increases which will be hard to accommodate without major problems of land and water scarcity. In these areas reproductive rights receive a very high priority.

Increasingly our concern must focus on consumption, and how we can cope with the effects of its inexorable increase. Over the past 25 years world population increased by 53 per cent, but world consumption per person (Measured by income) by only 39 per cent. Assume that consumption per person will rise 100 per cent, while population will rise by only half that amount. As time goes on the preponderance of consumption will increase more and more.

There is a crucial difference between population and consumption aspirations. If fully assured of children's survival most people have quite modest desires for family size. But their desire to consume knows no upper bounds. As wealth increases, people double-up their possessions; two or three cars, two bathrooms, two rooms with all contents, two or three holidays a year.

Appliances improve every year and old ones "need" replacing. New needs are created that never existed before. Globalisation is making products cheaper than ever. TVs are no longer uncommon even in African shanty towns. The number of households is increasing as people live longer and family breakdown becomes more common. Smaller households consume considerably more per cent than large. Moreover, consumption is politically very difficult to restrain. No one can get elected promising people they can earn and spend less, or re-elected if they fulfil their promises.

In view of this much of the burden of reducing our environmental impact will rest on technology. Technology will have to deliver major shifts in improving resource productivity, and in reducing the amount of waste we create. All our institutions and forms of management which affect technology will need to be geared to this end.

In some areas the record has been good and looks likely to remain so. Productivity has kept up with demand in the case of resources that are traded on markets, and that are under the direct control of people or companies affected by shortages or prices. Global food production has kept pace with demand: although land and cereal production per person has declined, average intakes of calories and protein have continued to improve and are at record levels. Malnutrition persists, but this is due to poverty and landlessness, not to the inability of the world to produce enough food. We have not encountered any limiting shortage of any key mineral resources or of energy. Nor are we likely to, because we continually economise and find substitutes, there has been a gradual reduction in the material used for each unit of production.

The prospects are much worse for resources that are not traded on markets or subject to sustainable management, as yet. These include groundwater, state forests, ocean fish, biodiversity in general. They include communal waste sinks like rivers, lakes and oceans, and the global atmosphere. In all of these areas it looks likely that things will get quite a lot worse before they get better.

These kinds of resources and sinks are not under the direct control of people affected by shortage or damage. People wishing to change the way a common resource or sink is used or managed have to pass through the legal or political system. They must organise, take out lawsuits against polluters, pressurise legislators and so on. Political responses are typically slow. Usually the majority of voters have to be convinced of the need for action before politicians will risk taking action. Even then powerful and rich vested interest will lobby hard for the status quo, and will often succeed in frustrating changes that are desired by a global majority. American's coal, oil, and car lobbies have stood in the way of any significant US commitment to reduce carbon dioxide output, and the US is the world's largest emitter of carbon dioxide.

Usually there has to be very widespread and very visible environmental damage before action is taken. The thinning of the ozone layer fitted that category well and the response was swift. North Atlantic fishing reached that point in the 1990s, yet politicians shied away from taking adequate action until the last moment: fishing stocks plummeted and there was massive job loss. Global warming is still long way from the damage being widespread enough, and attributable clearly enough to human activities, for politicians to be ready to speed up the move into renewable energy.

The question with the common resources and sinks is always: will we react in time? The answer is all the more difficult because we usually don't know in advance what is "in time." Many critical changes are subject to threshold effects. When a certain point is crossed, very sudden and disastrous change can occur with little warning. In many cases we do not know where the thresholds lie.

Prudence dictates a preventive approach—a stitch in time saves nine. But the history of environmental problems shows that politicians rarely act decisively until the brink is reached, and it will always be touch and go whether we are pushed over it or not.

Aid Effectiveness as a Multi-level Process

Parallel to the widespread decrease of aid resources provided by donor countries to developing countries in recent years, debate and research on how to make aid more effective has become a major concern. Usually, it is suggested that decades of development assistance have at best produced marginal results in terms of improving development levels in the South. Little mention is made of donor's policy shortcomings and the negative impact of these on efforts aimed at reforming and redefining development cooperation in order to enhance aid effectiveness. The policy parameters and operating frameworks of existing aid policies continue to inhibit higher degrees of aid effectiveness. In many donor countries, opinion polls indicate waning public support for development aid.

Increasingly, the moral case for aid is called into question and deeper world market integration tends to be seen as the panacea to continued economic decline and social destabilisation in the South. Against this background, cooperation between donor and recipient actors is faced with a duel uphill struggle. First, fewer resources can be mobilised to meet growing developmental needs. On the other hand, to organise and manage development policies and programmes in a result-oriented manner, grows more difficult. The threat of further aid cuts and of further drops of public support for providing aid become ever more real. A closer look at the organisational complexities and political constraints under which development cooperation is expected to perform effectively may help to improve current aid management approaches.

Towards Conceptual Clarity

At first sight, catchy definitions of what constitutes effective aid might appear attractive to use, in particular with regard to economic indicators. The term "aid effectiveness" is easily used in the same vein as "efficiency", "significance" or "impact" of aid. At times, obsession to measure and demonstrate the results of aid supported development processes can be observed among policy-makers and administrators on the donor side. Still the understanding of aid and its effectiveness as being part and parcel of a cooperation relationship between donor and recipient side parties, is scarcely embedded in practice. To determine how to make aid more effective requires more than a quick impact analysis of an individual and perhaps even isolated development project. Consequently, defining the concept of aid effectiveness needs to take into account at what levels cooperation is focused on. To strive for sustainable and effective modes of development cooperation will entail the need to combine recipient ownership of the development process with donor accountability concerns.

Performance expectations cannot be exclusively placed on the recipient while donor interests, their aid management systems and procedures remain unchanged.

An extended and more analytical, process-oriented definition should take into account four main aspects of aid effectiveness:

(a) Effective aid must relate to the building and/or strengthening of in-country aid management capacity;

(b) To maximise the degree of aid effectiveness, local ownership of the aid process is essential: from setting of priorities through policy formulation and implementation on to the evaluation stages of the process;

(c) Increasing recipient side capabilities to take charge of aid relationship, will need to be combined with arrangements to meet legitimate donor accountability concerns;

(d) Aid effectiveness is a two-faceted objective: its realisation is equally dependent on increased transparency of donor motives and on dropping of non-developmental, political and economic aid objectiveness of donors.

In addition a broader range of stakeholders in the aid relationship needs to be actively involved: extending beyond accountable government and implementing agencies, to include democratic institutions and organisations of civil society and of the private sector.

Applying any definition of aid effectiveness without disaggregating macro-economic data and taking into account country specificity will only lead to unhelpful generalisations about aid and its effectiveness. It would seem more appropriate to adopt working definitions against which to assess effectiveness of aid resources at a country-specific level. On such a basis one could expect to arrive at more reliable indicators of how well aid resources contribute to improving developmental standards and meeting existing needs.

From Definition to Success—Key Requirements

Having reached agreement between the recipient and donor on what should constitute effectiveness of aid is only a starting point. Embarking on democratic, peaceful and participatory patterns of economic and social development must follow: to arrive at significant and lasting improvement in many of the least developed countries will be a long-term process. This being said, it is crucial to design and implements such forms of development cooperation which involve a wide range of recipient side actors, not only from the government side but also from civil society at large. Seen as a process of increasing inclusion of intended beneficiaries of aid, the commitment to decentralise as well as entrust aid and its management grows in importance.

To fully capture Third World development realities, policy frameworks inspired by neoliberalist-type of development concepts and theories are grossly inadequate. The views and positions on aid articulated in the World Bank and the IMF, or in many if not most bilateral aid administrations in OECD countries, represent only one side of today's international cooperation, namely the donor side. The major weakness to point out with respect to this locus of debate, is a profound under representation if not even a total absence of recipient experiences and perceptions on aid in general and on its effectiveness in particular. There should be little doubt that ignoring to not actively identifying and involving such perceptions, leads to strongly donor driven aid.

To circumvent recipient side insights and views on strengths and weaknesses of aid strategies and mechanisms, will result in limited local commitment and sense of ownership over the aid process. Mutual decision-making between donors and recipients remains a rare policy approach. Aid procedures that are based on local management and less control-oriented donor roles in the aid process are still exceptions in development cooperation.

Structurally, in terms of the policy environment within which development aid is expected to function, the overriding policy framework is generally based on structural adjustment policies (SAP). But the underlying conclusion made by proponents of SAPs that these policies induce aid effectiveness, has yet to be proven valid. It must suffice at this point to emphasize that there is no *a priori* relationship between world market integration under structural adjustment and sustainable development in poor countries. Aid to these countries which is solely intended to reinforce fundamentally uneven and unequal patterns of world market integration should be scrutinised critically.

Some central issues need to be addressed in the course of improving aid and its effectiveness:

- institutional dimensions of aid relationships require strong policy-attention, both on the donor and the recipient side;
- capacities to effectively identify and formulate aid priorities need to be strengthened in recipient countries;
- local capacities to sustain reform efforts must be reinforced.

Levels of Intervention

If the design of aid and the terms upon which it is provided to a developing country are largely determined by the donor, the aid relationship can be characterised as essentially hierarchical. Recipient side views will rarely surface, as they are either not identified, or not well formulated. Possibilities of a recipient-led development strategies can be limited. Unless scope is provided to the recipient side actors to assume responsibilities, aid effectiveness is likely to remain low or fluctuating, and the sustainability of donor aid efforts will remain doubtful.

National planning processes and courses of national development in recipient countries should be seen as most effective where they are led under local responsibility and control. To arrive at this ideal situation, gaps need to be reduced and closed at the various intervention levels.

Donor aid resources provide valuable support for this process. Their effectiveness in meeting long-term objective of aid will need to be assessed on the basis of how well they perform at the different levels. Individual donors will expectedly perform differently at the various levels. What will prove to be the ultimate test for effectiveness is how well the donor aid performance accomplishes the broader objectives of development cooperation and how well it includes sustainable results.

In the analytical frameworks outlined here, development cooperation would seem to be confronted with the effectiveness gaps at the:

- *Structural Level:* International trade and investment patterns, debt problems and world market integration process appear as long-term constraining factors upon aid and its effectiveness;
- *Policy Level:* Dialogue and partnership in development cooperation are instrumental factors in recluding planning and co-ordination gaps with regard to policy analysis and formulation;
- The *Institutional Level* is where pertinent capacity gaps exist: capacity development efforts of donors and technical assistance measures play an important role in addressing weaknesses in aid effectiveness within a country's institutional setting;
- Finally, at the *level of aid projects* (programmes), it is generally the lack of sustainability of aid interventions which causes development activities to falter once donor support decreases or stops. In addition to technical cooperation, financial and material inputs serve to maintain project momentum and goal realisation. The issue of how to develop local capacity sufficiently in order for indigenous organisations to continue project activities initially supported by donor aid, remains the most important issue to address at this level.

Fostering Aid Effectiveness

Donor and recipient development efforts are too often isolated from one another, or poorly coordianted. They fail to address managerial and implementation bottlenecks. Cross-sectoral linkages, as well as interdisciplinary approaches to aid problems are only slowly gaining ground. It is increasingly obvious, that decisions on aid issues are subjected to concerns outside of the responsible ministry. Finance Ministers, and unfortunately even Defence Ministers have a strong say in how much aid is to be provided, where it is to be concentrated and under what terms to be utilised. Inside of recipient countries, large portions of national budgets are allocated to non-development priorities with little or no impact on alleviating urgent poverty problems.

Development cooperation may make the biggest impact and be executed most effectively where donors and recipients agree upon multi-level aid strategies. To give an example, building a road to a remote rural area may well be done in an effective project manner. It is equally important to have a functioning transport authority in place to ensure maintenance of the roads. If this authority operates within a nationally defined infrastructure policy, best in accord with national trade and investment priorities, then the effectiveness of the project-level road building programme has a good chance of being high.

Institutional changes to set the stage for a profound reform process in development cooperation are needed. Reprioritising national budgets to reflect identified in country development needs may be one step. Setting up policy evaluation and formulation units can be complimentary measures. Deregulating markets and investment rules may serve to please donors, but dumping of cheap products which strangle local production efforts may easily result. Regional cooperation, including intensified South-South cooperation can provide some counterbalance. There are only a few areas where changes in the current system of development cooperation can occur, with a view to better manage the complexities of aid and the social, cultural, economic and political backgrounds against which they take place. The will and commitment to take policy action in both donor and recipient countries, through the broadest range of stakeholders and institutions as possible, will be the test for genuine efforts at improving development relations between North and South and organising cooperation effectively.

Bibliography

De Soto, H., 1990. *The Other Path; The Invisible Revolution in the Third World,* Reprint edition. New York: Harper Collins.

Doha Development Agenda, 2001. *The Ministerial Declaration and other Decisions and Declarations from the Doha Ministerial Conference,* Available: http://www.wto.org/english/tratop_e/dda_e/dda_e.htm.

English, P., B. Hoekman, and A. Mattoo, 2002, *Development, Trade and the WTO: A Handbook.* The World Bank, Washington, D.C.

Feketekuty, G., 1988. *International Trade in Services: An Overview and Blueprint for Negotiations,* Cambridge, MA: American Enterprise Institute/Ballinger.

Finger, J.M., 1993. *Antidumping: How It Works and Who Gets Hurt.* Ann Arbor: Univ. of Michigan Press.

Finger, J.M., 2001. "Implementing the Uruguay Round Agreements: Problems for Developing Countries." *The World Economy* 24(9, September): 107-108.

Finger, J.M. and J.J. Nogues, 2001. The Unbalanced Uruguay Round Outcome: The New Areas in Future WTO Negotiations. *Policy Research Working Paper No. 2732,* The World Bank, Washington, D.C.

Finger, J.M. and L. Schuknecht, 2001. "Market Access Advances and Retreats: The Uruguay Round and Beyond." In B. Hoekman and W. Martin, eds., *Developing Countries and the WTO: A Pro-active Agenda.* Oxford: UK and Malden. Also available as Policy Research Working Paper No. 2232 at http://www.worldbank.org/research/trade.

Finger, J.M. and P. Schuler, 2000. "Implementation of Uruguay Round Commitments: The Development Challenge." *The World Economy* 23(4, April): 511-25. Also available as Policy Research Working Paper No. 2215 at http://www.worldbank.org/research/trade.

Finger, J.M. and L.A. Winters, 2002. "Reciprocity." In P. English, B. Hoekman, and A. Mattoo, *Development, Trade and the WTO: A Handbook*. The World Bank, Washington, D.C.

Finger, J.M., M.D. Ingco, and U. Reincke, 1996. *The Uruguay Round: Statistics on Tariif Concessions Given and Received*. The World Bank, Washington, D.C.

Finger, J.M., F. Ng, and S. Wangchuk, 2001. Antidumping as Safeguard Policy. Policy Research Working Paper No. 2730, The World Bank, Washington, D.C.

Francois, J.F.,B. McDonald, and H. Nordstrom, 1996. "The Uruguay Round: A Numerically Based Qualitative Assessment." In W. Martin and L.A. Winters, eds., *The Uruguay Round and the Developing Countries*. Cambridge: Cambridge University Press.

Harrison, G.W., T.F. Rutherford, and D.G. Tarr, 1996. "Quantifying the Uruguay Round." In W. Martin and L.A. Winters, eds., *The Uruguay Round and the Developing Countries*. Cambridge: Cambridge University Press.

Hudec, R.E., 1970. "The GATT Legal System: A Diplomat's Jurisprudence." *Journal of World Trade Law* 4:615-65.

International Intellectual Property Alliance (IIPA), 2002a. "Description of the IIPA." Available: http://www.iipa.com/aboutiipa.html.

International Intellectual Property Alliance (IIPA), 2002b. "Statistics."Available: http://www.iipa.com/statistics.html.

Martin, W. and L.A. Winters, 1996. *The Uruguay Round and the Developing Countries*. Cambridge; Cambridge University Press.

Martin, W and L.A. Winters, 1996. "The Uruguay Round: a Milestone for the Developing Countries." In W. Martin and L.A. Winters, eds., *The Uruguay Round and the Developing Countries.* Cambridge: Cambridge University Press.

Maskus, K.E., 2000. *Intellectual Property Rights in the Global Economy.* Institute for International Economics, Washington, D.C.

Michalopoulos, C., 1999. "The Developing Countries in the WTO." *The World Economy* 22(1) January.

O'Neill, T. and G. Hymel (contributor), 1995, *All Politics is Local: And Other Rules of the Game.* Reprint edition. Massachusetts: Adams Media Corporation.

Panagariya, A., forthcoming. "Developing Countries at Doha: A Political Economy Analysis." *The World Economy.*

Petersen, M. and D.G. McNeil Jr., 2001. "Maker Yielding Patent in Africa for AIDS Drug" *The New York Times,* 15 March. p. 1.

Preeg, E.H., 1995. *Traders in a Brave New World.* Chicago and London: University of Chicago Press.

Reichman, J.H., 1998. "Securing Compliance with the TRIPS Agreement after US v India." *Journal of International Economic Law* 1(4, December): 603-06.

Ricupero, R., 2000. "A Development Round: Converting Rhetoric into Substance." Paper Presented at the Symposium on Efficiency, Equity and Legitimacy: The Multilateral Trading System at the Millennium, 1-2 June, John F. Kennedy School of Government, Harvard University, Cambridge, Massachusetts.

Shaffer, G., 2002. "The Law-in Action of International Trade Litigation: The Blurring of the Public and the Private." University of Wisconsin Law School, Madison Manuscript.

Winham, G., 1986. *International Trade and The Tokyo Round of Negotiations.* Princeton: Princeton University Press.

Winters, L.A., 2002. "Doha and the World Poverty Targets." Paper Prepared for the Annual Bank Conference on Development Economics (ABCDE), 29-30 April, World Bank, Washington, D.C.

World Bank, 2002, *Global Economic Prospects and the Developing Countries*. The World Bank, Washington D.C.

World Trade Organisation (WTO), 2002a. "WTO Secretariat Budget for 2002." Available: http://www.wto.org/english/thewto_e/secre_e/budget _e.htm.

World Trade Organisation (WTO), 2002b. Pledging Conference to provide sound financial basis for Doha Agenda. Available: http://www.wto.org./english/news_e/pres02_e/pr277_e.htm.

Zeller, T.W., 1992. *American Trade and Power in the 1960s*. New York: Columbia.

INDEX

Z